SUPERPOWER

Three Choices for America's Role in the World

IAN BREMMER

PORTFOLIO
PENGUIN

PORTFOLIO PENGUIN

UK | USA | Canada | Ireland | Australia
India | New Zealand | South Africa

Portfolio Penguin is part of the Penguin Random House group of companies
whose addresses can be found at global.penguinrandomhouse.com

First published in the United States of America by Portfolio/Penguin, an imprint of
Penguin Publishing Group, a division of Penguin Random House LLC 2015
First published in Great Britain by Portfolio Penguin 2015
This paperback edition with a new preface by Ian Bremmer published 2016
001

Printed in Great Britain by Clays Ltd, St Ives plc

A CIP catalogue record for this book is available from the British Library

ISBN: 978–0–241–24732–7

www.greenpenguin.co.uk

MIX
Paper from
responsible sources
FSC® C018179

Penguin Random House is committed to a
sustainable future for our business, our readers
and our planet. This book is made from Forest
Stewardship Council® certified paper.

To Willis

Contents

CONTENTS

Preface

The world is fast becoming a much more dangerous place, and the question of how America should respond is hotly debated both at home and abroad. In the months since this book appeared in hardcover, the list of game-changing international news stories has only grown longer. China spooked the entire global economy in August 2015, and again in January 2016, when its benchmark Shanghai stock exchange seemed to be in free fall. A corruption investigation in Brazil panicked half its elected officials and up-ended the government. The wave of Middle Eastern refugees headed north and west toward Europe rose to new heights, ISIS raged on. Suicide bombings shifted the course of politics in Turkey. Russia joined the roster of combatants in Syria, its first military campaign outside former Soviet territory since the Cold War's end, and then a Russian passenger plane exploded over Egypt. Days later, Paris suffered its deadliest terrorist attack in decades. As of this writing, Britain stands on the verge of a vote that will determine its future as a member of the European Union.

None of these developments threatened the United States directly. The U.S. economy continues its postcrisis recovery. Unemployment has fallen. The long wars in Iraq and Afghanistan are mostly over (at least as far as the United States is concerned). The United States is now the world's number one producer of oil and natural gas. The impact of illegal immigration into the United States is nothing like the costs and risks facing Europe as governments and citizens struggle to cope with a million more Muslim migrants and the pressure they exert on local politics and Europe's open borders. The Western Hemisphere remains the world's most peaceful and stable region.

But though Americans can afford to watch the troubles of others from afar, at least for now, many of these conflicts expose the increasingly obvious limits of U.S. international influence. Washington seems unable to help manage the world's emergencies. What should the next U.S. president do about that? Should he/she develop a comprehensive strategy to ensure that democracy and freedom shape the emerging world order? Or is it the next president's responsibility to take on new international risks and responsibilities only where and when it's clear that Washington can strengthen U.S. security and prosperity? Or maybe it's time to accept, at least temporarily, that U.S. interests are best served by redirecting resources now devoted to a superhero foreign policy toward America's future by investing at home. All of these choices have strengths and weaknesses, but it's crucial for Americans to choose a single coherent approach if we are to make best use of our limited resources. Events of the past six months have only made that choice a more urgent one.

Barack Obama has achieved some noteworthy things. The

Trans-Pacific Partnership, the nuclear deal with Iran, and a diplomatic breakthrough with Cuba could all produce positive lasting results. But accomplishments alone don't suggest a broader foreign policy strategy under construction or that Americans now better understand which responsibilities their country can and cannot afford to accept. Obama was elected in part to end the wars in Iraq and Afghanistan without starting any new ones. The public has generally supported his cautious approach to military commitments. But the next president will have a much wider range of questions to answer.

Choosing the next president has been a particularly contentious process. The 2016 election has indeed become a referendum on America's approach to the rest of the world. It has raised fundamental questions about burden-sharing with our allies, about when, where, and why we send troops overseas, about what it means to be the world's most influential democracy and its largest free market economy.

Donald Trump and Bernie Sanders, fist-shaking populists with little experience of, or interest in, foreign policy, made most of the headlines in 2016, often with verbal assaults on (what they say are) free-riding allies. Both men gripe that Washington pays too big a percentage of NATO's bills. They agree that recent trade deals have cheated the American worker, though they explain the problem differently. Trump says that weak-kneed U.S. negotiators have made bad deals in recent years that allowed China, Mexico, Japan, and other countries to steal U.S. jobs and growth. Sanders counters that U.S. dealmakers are far from incompetent. Instead, they're elites making deals with other elites to benefit elites. Both men's views are grounded in resentment and suspicion.

But it's Trump who has fundamentally changed the debate. He has no foreign policy experience, but he does have a coherent worldview, and conservative voters responded to it. It's an approach I labeled "America First" during an interview in early 2016, without meaning it as a compliment, and I was more than a little surprised when Trump liked that formulation enough to adopt it for his campaign.[1] (Irony alert: I sent copies of the hardback version of this book to every campaign except his. Serves me right for being so wrong about his chances of winning the Republican nomination.)

Trump has offered a hyper-nationalist approach to foreign policy. Bomb ISIS into oblivion. Take the oil. Build a wall and make Mexico pay for it. Ban Muslims from the country. Stop acting like chumps. Threaten China, Mexico, and Japan with a trade war unless they give us more of what we want. Abandon alliances when allies don't pay their fair share. No one can say this isn't a strong view of America's role in the world. It's the clearest possible repudiation of the idea that Americans have a special responsibility to promote, protect, and defend democracy and freedom beyond U.S. borders. It's grounded in the conviction that Washington can and should refuse to enter into agreements of any kind with any government that refuses to negotiate on the president's terms.

That message resonates with Americans who have become increasingly skeptical that the world wants U.S. leadership—and, more important, that Washington's international leadership benefits Americans. Many older voters worry that America has become a fundamentally different country than the one they were taught to be proud of, and younger voters didn't grow up with Cold War–era assumptions about the need for America to lead. Political polarization between conservatives and progressives of all ages has intensified. Protests have grown angrier and uglier. All these factors make it more difficult for any president, elected by half the country, to build consensus for any coherent, long-term view of America's role in tomorrow's world. But without that consensus, we could see the disintegration of everything Americans have helped build since the end of World War II.

Outside of Trump and Sanders, most of the 2016 presidential candidates limited their foreign policy pronouncements to predictably broad generalizations. Republicans were eager to talk foreign policy as a means of attacking Hillary Clinton's record as Obama's secretary of state. But when asked whether and how they might use U.S. power in the Middle East or in response to China's rise or Russian aggression, most of them fell back on empty boasts and boilerplate blah blah blah about America's timeless greatness. They refused to acknowledge limits, risks, costs, or the sometime virtues of cooperation and compromise. Their speeches were the rhetorical equivalent of American flag lapel pins. Talk loudly and wave a huge stick. Rip up the Iran deal. Put Putin in his place. Let the Chinese know who's boss. The massacre in San Bernadino, California, that closed 2015 reminded us that future terrorist attacks are less likely to unite the country, as after 9/11, but to divide the nation along partisan lines. Populist grandstanding increases the risk of reckless responses to challenges that demand careful thought.

Grandstanding wins applause. It sometimes wins votes. But it can never become the basis for a coherent foreign policy. There are also some Republicans who prefer a more hands-off approach on these issues, but staying out of the way while your enemies fight one another doesn't offer long-term solutions to chronic foreign-policy problems. The debate can't simply be whether America should lead or stand on the sidelines. The larger questions of how, why, and toward what end must be answered.

Hillary Clinton tried hard to avoid the subject of foreign policy during debates with Bernie Sanders because, beyond highlighting his inexperience, she saw no clear electoral advantage in talking about it. In particular, she remained extraordinarily evasive about her views on trade. While Trump and Sanders made it very clear where they stand, Clinton tried to have it both ways. As Obama's secretary of state, she praised the enormous Trans-Pacific Partnership as the "gold standard" in international trade. Then, while running for president, her bid to triangulate Bernie Sanders out of the race led her to argue that details of the deal prevented her from supporting it.

There are good reasons for candidates to avoid policy specifics that can be distorted in ways that cost them votes, and a future president does the country no favors by telling others exactly how he or she would try to solve this intractable problem or respond to that hypothetical crisis. But presidential candidates too often refuse to explain their most basic assumptions about how best to make America safer and more prosperous. There are exceptions. During a Republican debate in November 2015, Senators Rand Paul and Marco Rubio dove into an interesting argument. Here's an edited version of their exchange:

MARCO RUBIO: I know that [Senator] Rand [Paul] is a committed isolationist. I'm not. I believe the world is a stronger and a better place when the United States is the strongest military power in the world.

RAND PAUL: Yeah, but, Marco, how is it conservative to add a trillion-dollar expenditure for the federal government that you're not paying for? You cannot be a conservative if you're going to keep promoting new programs that you're not going to pay for.

(APPLAUSE)

RUBIO: We can't even have an economy if we're not safe. There are radical jihadists in the Mid-

dle East beheading people and crucifying
Christians. A radical Shia cleric in Iran trying to get a nuclear weapon. The Chinese
taking over the South China Sea. . . . I know
that the world is a safer place when America
is the strongest military power in the world.
(CHEERING AND APPLAUSE)

PAUL: I do not think we are any safer from bank-
ruptcy court. As we go further and further
into debt, we become less and less safe. This
is the most important thing we're going to
talk about tonight. Can you be a conservative and be liberal on military spending?
Can you be for unlimited military spending
and say, "Oh, I'm going to make the country
safe"? We spend more on our military than
the next ten countries combined? I want a
strong national defense, but I don't want us
to be bankrupt.

There are a lot of phony debates out there about foreign policy,
which usually involve someone railing against an opinion that no
one actually holds. But there are plenty of real debates too, and this
is a good example. Is a superpower foreign policy bankrupting
America, wasting taxpayer dollars in places like Iraq and Afghanistan, money that's better spent at home or left in the taxpayer's
pocket? Or is it foolish to believe that America can be secure and
prosperous if the world's fires are allowed to burn out of control?
This is an argument with forceful points on both sides.

There are many more questions that deserve serious debate. How
should the United States respond to the next stage of China's rise at a

time when it's using its more than $3 trillion dollars in financial reserves to extend its economic influence? How important for the United States is the trans-Atlantic relationship? Is an ambitious new trade deal with Europe a good idea? Should the United States accept more of the world's refugees? As the Middle East becomes more dangerously unstable, should Washington become more directly involved? If so, how and to what end? Can Washington really destroy ISIS? Can it afford not to? Is there anything the United States can and should do to improve relations with Russia or contain Vladimir Putin's revanchist ambitions? How valuable are traditional partnerships with old friends like Britain, Japan, and Israel? What approach should Washington take toward Iran? And Saudi Arabia? Is it wise to become more actively involved in political disputes in Latin America and sub-Saharan Africa? Should the next president follow up on Obama's opening to Cuba? None of these questions can be answered in isolation. Each response will depend on the answer to a larger question: What role should America play in this new world?

These are among the many important questions I'll ask you to consider in the pages that follow as you decide for yourself how America should use its superpower. The 2016 presidential campaign hasn't addressed any of these questions in a serious way. That's a missed opportunity—for Americans and for everyone else. The world is changing much more quickly than U.S. presidential candidates would lead voters to believe, and the next international crisis, whatever it is and wherever it hits, is likely to be more complicated and involve more dangerous choices than Americans expect.

Ian Bremmer
New York City
May 9, 2016

SUPERPOWER

Introduction

We are our choices.
—Jean-Paul Sartre

America will remain the world's only superpower for the fore-seeable future. But what sort of superpower should it be? What role should America play in the world? What role do you *want* America to play?

Some say the time has come for the United States to mind its own business, let other countries solve their own problems, and focus instead on rebuilding America's strength from within. Others insist that Washington can and should pursue an ambitious foreign policy, but one designed solely to make America more secure and more prosperous, not to foist our political and economic values on others. Still others say the world needs leadership and that only America can provide it. They argue that Americans and everyone else will be better off if democracy, freedom of speech, access to information, and the rights of the individual are universally respected.

What do you think? To help you decide, have a go at the following ten questions. Choose the single answer that best represents your opinion.

1. Freedom is:

    a. The right of every human being.

    b. Fragile. Americans must protect it right here at home.

    c. In the eye of the beholder.

2. America is:

    a. Exceptional because of what it represents.

    b. Exceptional because of all it has done for the world.

    c. Not an exceptional nation. America is the most powerful, but that doesn't mean it's always right.

3. Which of these statements best expresses your opinion?

    a. America will be better off if we mind our own business and let other countries get along the best they can.

    b. America must lead.

    c. The primary purpose of U.S. foreign policy should be to make America safer and more prosperous.

4. China is:

    a. America's greatest challenge and greatest opportunity.

    b. The place where too many American jobs have gone.

    c. The world's largest dictatorship.

5. America's biggest problem in the Middle East is that:

   a. Washington supports the region's dictators rather than its people.

   b. Washington ignores small problems until they turn into big ones.

   c. Washington believes it can manage an unmanageable region.

6. U.S. spy capabilities:

   a. Will always be a double-edged sword.

   b. Threaten our privacy.

   c. Are vital for protecting America.

7. The primary responsibility of the president of the United States is:

   a. To advance U.S. interests at home and abroad.

   b. To promote, protect, and defend the Constitution of the United States.

   c. To lead.

8. Which of the following best expresses your view?

   a. A great leader can change the world.

   b. A great leader must lead by example.

   c. In the real world, any leader must often choose the least bad of many bad options.

9. Which is the most at risk?

    a. America's economy.

    b. America's international reputation.

    c. The respect of our leaders for America's founding principles.

10. I hope that by the year 2050:

    a. America will share the burdens of leadership with reliable, like-minded allies.

    b. Americans will have created a more perfect union at home.

    c. American leadership will have helped as many people as possible around the world topple the tyrants who deny them the freedom they deserve.

We'll come back to these questions in the conclusion, and I promise to tell you exactly what I believe and why I believe it—and I'll refer back to this quiz at the end of chapters 3, 4, and 5. But this book is about what *you* think. Whether you're an American or the proud citizen of another country, I want to know what role you believe the world's only superpower should play in our world. If you finish the book with a strong opinion, especially if it's a bit different than the one you have at this moment, and even if it's the opposite of mine, this book will have served its purpose.

I'm proud to be a political scientist, one who takes seriously his responsibility to offer unbiased analysis. I'm also intensely proud to be an American. You should know that right at the top. Among my ancestors are men and women from Armenia, Italy, Syria, Germany, and the Native American tribes that made their way across Central Asia, the Bering Strait, and the great North American plains. I grew up in the projects of Chelsea, Massachusetts, where I felt completely at home on my mainly Puerto Rican Little League baseball team, in my heavily Italian high school, and among the mainly Anglo middle-class kids I knew in my Junior Achievement group. Beyond the melting pot, my patriotism is an inevitable product of my childhood. My father died when I was four. My mother raised me and my brother with little help, little money, and unshakable confidence that a good education and a lot of hard work would give me the chance to invent my own future.

Because I love my country, I feel a responsibility to honor its virtues and accomplishments and to think and write about its shortcomings. I also care very much about America's place in the world—what it is, what it could be, and what it should be. I want my country to find the courage to help others solve problems and the wisdom to avoid creating new ones. I also love a debate. Not the ones where politicians preen and bob and weave while pundits tally up their applause lines and verbal stumbles. I love debates in which brave and sincere men and women take up serious subjects in hopes of opening new doors onto undiscovered country. That's the kind of debate America needs right now.

Parts of this book are centered on international turmoil and our world in transition—European fears, Russian ambitions, Middle East dangers, and Chinese riddles. But as you'll see, it's not about big global trends that Americans can't control: the rise and fall of nations, emerging-world economics, or a disintegrating global order. Nor is it about blame for past mistakes. It's about America's role in tomorrow's world and the choices we must begin to make as the next round of presidential candidates—Republicans, Democrats, and maybe a wild card or two—ask us for money, support, and our votes.

In chapter 1, I'll write about today's world, America's limits, and its opportunity to transcend them. In chapter 2, I'll briefly detail the incoherence of America's post–Cold War foreign policy. In the next three chapters, I'll outline three distinctly different choices for our future, three conflicting arguments on what role America should play in this world in transition. Not all the opinions expressed in these chapters reflect my personal views. How could they? They represent directly competing visions of America's future. But I've done my best in each chapter to put forth the strongest arguments I can, and I ask you to decide which one you think is the most persuasive.

Chapter 3, "Independent America," will try to persuade you that it's time for America to declare independence from the need to solve other people's problems and to finally realize our country's enormous untapped potential by focusing our attentions at home. Chapter 4, "Moneyball America," will argue that important parts of chapter 3 are dangerous nonsense, that there are a few things in this world that must be done, and that it's in America's interest for Americans to do them. Chapter 5, "Indispensable America," will insist that these other two visions of our country's future are unworthy of a great nation, that America can never establish lasting security and prosperity in the interconnected modern world until we have helped others win their freedom, and that we must keep our eyes on this prize even if it takes a hundred years to achieve. In chapter 6, I'll detail why all three of these choices have strengths and flaws, but I'll also argue that refusing to choose is the worst choice of all.

When I began writing this book, I didn't know which of these three choices I would favor. It's easy to be swayed by pundits and politicians with a story to sell or an ax to grind. My attempt to make the most honest and forceful case I could make for each of these three arguments helped me understand what I believe and why I believe it. I hope it will do the same for you. But I'll wait until the conclusion to tell you what I *really* think. And I'll remind you again that I don't ask you to agree with me.

I ask only that you choose.

CHAPTER 1
Today's World and Tomorrow's

A pessimist sees the difficulty in every opportunity;
an optimist sees the opportunity in every difficulty.
—Winston Churchill

Our world is always in transition, but there are historical moments when the death of the existing order and the violent birth of a new one create extraordinary turmoil. This is one of those moments. The United States remains the world's only military superpower, but costly, ill-conceived nation-building projects in Iraq and Afghanistan and the inability to resolve more recent conflicts leave Americans cynical about the value of U.S. power and reluctant to test it anywhere else. The great financial meltdown of 2008 led some to question whether the U.S. economy still stands on a firm foundation, and in the years that followed, stock prices recovered but the U.S. job market did not prove quite as resilient. America's allies in Europe, the Middle East, East Asia, and elsewhere now question the strength of Washington's commitment to the global responsibilities it claimed for itself in better days. Rivals and adversaries see new opportunities to test American intentions.

In recent years, emerging powers like China, Russia, the Gulf Arab leaders, India, Brazil, Turkey, and others have proven that they can reject U.S. leadership where it isn't useful for them and extend their influence within their own regions. Yet governments in all these countries now face complex domestic challenges, leaving them unwilling and unable to offer a real alternative to that leadership. The U.S.-dominated post–Cold War order has come to an end. We now live in a world where no single power or alliance of powers can offer consistent global leadership. No one knows what comes next.

The breakdown of the old order has stirred up a remarkable amount of trouble over the past seven years. After the crash of once-formidable U.S. banks created extreme financial turbulence and a global recession, the Eurozone spiraled into crisis. The Middle East erupted. Well-organized and -financed Islamic radicals launched bold new attacks on the modern world. Fault lines began to appear among power players at the highest level of China's leadership and, not coincidentally, Beijing began to pursue a much more aggressive foreign policy. Russia and the West again found themselves in conflict. Many of these fires will burn for years to come.

Consider the high-stakes questions facing America's next president. Begin with the many risks created by changing times in China, a country whose social stability and economic vital signs have become crucial for the health of the entire global economy. As I'll detail in later chapters, China's leaders have staked their future on a long-term reform process designed to help the country finally make the leap from a poor one that sells consumer goods to America, Europe, and Japan to a modern one driven by an expanding middle class with the cash to buy more of the products China makes. They must help develop a more innovative economy, one fueled by efficient, dynamic private-sector firms rather than corrupt, inefficient state-owned dinosaurs. China's companies must master new technologies that produce energy and growth without continued catastrophic damage to the country's air and water. Its policymakers must manage the widening gap between the urban rich and rural poor. And they must do all this to extend the ruling party's monopoly hold on political power for another generation.

But Beijing's reformers are under pressure—from upwardly mobile urban Chinese tired of promises and ready for change, from factory workers who fear that these changes will cost them their jobs, and from some of the country's wealthiest, best-connected power brokers who know these changes will strip them of privileges and protections. In response to these pressures, President Xi Jinping has launched an ambitious anticorruption campaign that has already taken down some of China's most powerful people, in order to push aside opponents of reform and to earn greater trust from a cynical Chinese public. Over time, this strategy will provoke greater pushback from threatened officials who feel they have nothing to lose, raising the odds that a fight within the leadership will spill into the open, generating frightening levels of unrest across the country. All this at a time when ideas and information travel into, out of, and across China at greater speed than ever before in history. This reality increases the odds that no matter what Washington does, turmoil inside China will throw the entire global economy into reverse.

The next American president must also prepare for the day when trouble across China pushes Beijing toward conflict with its neighbors, including U.S. allies, via acts of aggression meant to distract China's people from the failings of their government. To assert its fast-expanding regional influence and appease demand, particularly within the military, for a more assertive foreign policy, Beijing has already become more confrontational, particularly in the region's disputed waters. This situation could become much more dangerous in coming years, because Japanese prime minister Shinzo Abe has announced plans to "reinterpret" Japan's constitution to allow his country to move its security policy beyond self-defense. This change makes it more likely that China and Japan will more often confront one another in the East China Sea. The governments of the world's second- and third-largest economies will work hard to avoid a mutually costly military confrontation, but neither is deaf to domestic public demand for an uncompromising stand when tempers flare. If China one day becomes unstable, China, Japan, and America might quickly find themselves on a collision course through uncharted waters.

Next on the agenda is the conflict that again pits Russia against the West. This is not a new Cold War. Russia lacks the Soviet Union's international allies, ideological appeal, and military muscle. But a struggle that began in the streets of Kiev will continue to be fought in and around Ukraine; at Russia's borders with other neighbors; in energy markets, financial markets, the defense budgets of countries on both sides; and even in cyberspace. America's NATO allies—the former Soviet republics Estonia, Latvia, Lithuania, and former Warsaw Pact member Poland, in particular—will remain on alert for years. Estonia and Latvia are home to a larger percentage of ethnic Russians even than Ukraine, a lasting point of tension. A troubled history with Russia and the anger stoked by the fight for Ukraine makes Poland the most aggressively anti-Kremlin voice in Europe.

Further feeding the anxiety are Eastern European fears that

Russia cares much more about the future of its former communist allies than Western Europe or America ever will and that Moscow will fight harder and longer to preserve its influence in Ukraine than Washington, Brussels, or Berlin will defend Ukraine's right to self-determination. Vladimir Putin is convinced that the West is not committed to a long-term fight. He may well be right. Washington is also right to worry that this conflict is already driving energy-rich Russia and energy-thirsty China much closer together, a fear that will intensify if instability in China moves Beijing to try to shift public anger over reform toward anti-American fury.

The next president must also worry over the health of U.S. relations with the country's allies. In particular, the ties that bind Europe and the United States represent the most powerful potential coalition of capable and like-minded allies the world has ever known, but the transatlantic alliance is under increasingly serious stress. First, there are difficult and growing divisions within Europe itself. Demands from wealthier states like Germany for belt tightening and other painful economic reforms in Greece, Spain, Portugal, Italy, and even France have generated plenty of public anger in those countries. The impatience on all sides is obvious in elections for the European Parliament, where voters have cast an unprecedented number of ballots in recent years for anti-EU parties. Further dividing Europe are sharply differing opinions on the wisdom of confrontation with Russia.

Then there are the sources of division between Europe and the United States. The two sides agree on the need to beat back threats from Islamic radicals—though not always on how to do it—but they will never fully align on how best to handle Russia. The United States is not particularly vulnerable to blowback from bad relations with Moscow. In 2014, U.S. goods exports to Russia totaled just $11 billion and imports from Russia came to $24 billion. Russia is not among America's twenty largest trade partners.[1] For Europe, the stakes are much higher. Russia is the EU's third-biggest trade partner, importing €103.2 billion of goods from the EU in 2014. Russian exports to the EU totaled €182.4 billion that year.[2] Germany and most Eastern European countries will need substantial volumes of Russian energy for the foreseeable future. Slow-growth France needs Russian defense contracts. Britain needs Russian financial clients. This may become a source of serious U.S.-EU tension in coming years.

Nor does it help transatlantic relations that the U.S. National Security Agency has been caught spying on America's allies, raising fears across Europe that U.S. information technology firms have given the country's intelligence agencies deep access to European secrets. In response, German chancellor Angela Merkel took the extraordinary step in 2014 of calling for a European Internet that is walled off from the United States.[3] Anti-American anger in many European countries, which rose sharply during the presidency of George W. Bush, then eased with the election of Barack Obama, has surged back to life, making it more difficult for America's next president to win support from European governments for anything that wary European voters might not like.

America's next president must also figure what to do—and what not to do—about an increasingly volatile Middle East, where a growing number of bloody battles threaten to become one big war. War-weary Americans and reluctant-to-lead Europeans must weigh whether and how to engage ever more anxious Saudi Arabia, newly assertive Iran, fragile Iraq, authoritarian Egypt, and internally divided Turkey, and must manage the intractable, eternal struggle between Israelis and Palestinians. Making matters more dangerous, many radical Islamists no longer believe that the wave of change that swept away dictators in Egypt, Libya, Yemen, and

Tunisia and provoked unrest in other countries across North Africa and the Middle East during the so-called Arab Spring can help them use elections to bring about change. Instead, they've taken up arms, hoping to achieve by bloodshed what can't be won through politics.

In particular, the conquest of some of Iraq's largest cities in 2014 allowed the so-called Islamic State to become the best-financed terrorist organization in history, and the group continues to attract willing recruits from around the world looking for a fight to make their own. In Iraq, Syria, Mali, Nigeria, Libya, Tunisia, Yemen, and Somalia, holy war has begun to burn bright. Upping the ante for America's next leader, the region has become a training ground for Muslim radicals with European and U.S. passports, increasing alert levels in Western capitals. This threat, not the one jihad poses to the region's oil production, will be the most important problem that the Middle East creates for Americans in years to come.

Now look to the broader picture, because the tests awaiting the next president are larger than those from any one war zone, country, or region. Over the next generation, the global economy will depend more for its dynamism on the strength and resilience of emerging-market countries. That should worry us, because these countries are inherently less stable than the rich-world powers that have driven growth over the past several decades. These are places where, as in India in 2012, a government's failure to address infrastructure problems can trigger a blackout across an area that's home to 670 million people.[4] Or, as in Brazil in 2013, a nine-cent increase in bus fares in São Paulo can spark protests that drive a million people into the streets of major cities, and a lack of rainfall can generate an electricity shortage severe enough to push a country of 200 million people into recession.[5] Or, as in Turkey in 2013, an aggressive police response to protests over a plan to replace a grove of sycamore trees with a shopping mall can push 2 million angry people into demonstrations across the country.[6] It's entirely possible that during the next U.S. president's term in office, China will become the world's largest economy. What will it mean for global economic stability when the world economy is led by a still-poor, potentially unstable, authoritarian power?

An American president facing so much uncertainty and so many sources of potential trouble might be only too happy to share the burdens of leadership with willing partners, but who will step forward to help? Europe's leaders have their hands full with the internal struggle over how best to restore confidence in the Eurozone's long-term vitality and the security challenges posed by Putin's Russia. And they're unsure whether to make long-term economic bets on traditional ties and improved trade relations with America or hedge their bets by investing in a promising new partnership with rising China.

Japan, China, and India are unlikely to offer much international leadership, at least for the moment. Political leaders in all three countries are overwhelmingly focused on complicated, long-term economic reform projects. Japan's leaders must build on Prime Minister Shinzo Abe's bid to jump-start the country's growth by moving forward with controversial plans to allow more women and immigrants to bolster Japan's shrinking workforce. China's leaders must undertake an enormously complex economic restructuring that shifts vast amounts of wealth from state-run companies to Chinese consumers, to relieve the country's dependence for growth on exports to wealthy foreigners by empowering Chinese consumers to buy a larger share of Chinese-made products. They must enable market forces to make state-owned companies stronger and leaner. They must empower growth that allows for cleaner air and water. And they must overcome resistance to all these plans from wealthy, well-connected Chinese political and business leaders with much to lose from these changes. India's prime minister, Narendra Modi, wants to open long-protected economic sectors to foreign competition in order to develop the robust, competitive economy India needs to extend its regional and international influence. All these governments face extraordinary tests at home, and none of them is eager to accept the costs and risks that come with a greater share of global leadership, particularly when Washington still seems willing to do so much of the heavy lifting.

The greatest challenge facing the next president comes not from any one of these questions but from all of them together—and from a lack of consensus at home on how much or how little to do about them. Following the financial crisis, the United States, Europe, China, Japan, India, the Gulf Arabs, and others joined forces to take concrete steps that helped avoid a total collapse of the global financial system, but only because all these major powers felt threatened by the same risk at the same moment and to more or less the same degree.[7] Today's shift in the global balance of power and the trouble it's creating around the world don't pose the same sort of obvious, immediate, universal threat, and there is little hope for a unified international response.

The next president must recognize that the American people are exhausted by calls for intervention in foreign conflicts they don't understand. They want their elected leaders to get things done at home, help get Americans back to work, empower U.S. companies to compete more effectively, rebuild the country's strength from within, and restore confidence in America's future. That will require tough choices on the future of the country's role in the world. President Obama has consistently refused to try to build public support for an ambitious superpower foreign policy. But he has also refused to admit we must do more with less by setting a few priorities and sticking to them. And he has refused to redefine America's responsibilities by making clear that Washington will no longer play the role that others expect and that other governments will have to step forward and do more.

In short, Obama has refused to choose. His inability or unwillingness to build a foreign policy on any one of these three foundations, to lay the groundwork for a more coherent U.S. approach to the rest of the world, has added to America's problems both at home and abroad.

U.S. Foreign Policy Is in Decline . . .

Not that the decline of U.S. foreign policy is all Obama's fault. As I'll detail in the next chapter, the post–Cold War confusion and miscalculations extend back to the final fall of the Iron Curtain. Democrats and Republicans, presidents and lawmakers, deserve blame. Whoever is at fault, it's clear that America's next president will inherit a foreign policy without a strategy. The United States will remain the world's most formidable military power for decades to come. The gap between U.S. and Chinese defense spending grows wider in America's favor every day.[8] Only the United States can project military strength in every region of the world, in part because it owns more than half of the world's aircraft carriers.[9] Some say the real percentage is nearly two-thirds.[10]

But power is a measure of one's ability to force someone to do something he wouldn't otherwise do, and there are a growing number of governments today with the resources and self-confidence they need to simply say no. There was never a golden age of American power when everyone followed America's lead. Even at the height of the Cold War, U.S. allies often defied Washington's wishes.[11] But the United States is now less able to convene a coalition, forge trade agreements, build support for sanctions, broker compromise on an important multinational dispute, or persuade others to follow it into conflict than at any time in the past seven decades. Europeans are now less dependent on the United States for their security. China, Russia, India, Brazil, Turkey, and the Arab monarchs of the Persian Gulf can't change the global status quo on their own, but they have more than enough leverage to obstruct U.S. plans they don't like. Aware that Washington is focused on domestic priorities and that most Americans want no part of problems that don't immediately threaten U.S. national security, it doesn't take much to discourage direct U.S. intervention in Ukraine, Syria, or the South China Sea.

Adding to the dispersion of power, it's not just that there are now more diplomats at the world's bargaining tables. It's that these new players represent governments with differing political and economic values. There was never a day when the G7 group of industrialized countries ruled the world. But before the rise of China, India, Russia, Brazil, Turkey, and others over the past fifteen years, the United States, Japan, Britain, France, Germany, Italy, and Canada still held considerable collective sway. There was never a need during G7 summits to debate the value of democracy, freedom of speech, or free-market capitalism. Multinational institutions created by the United States and its allies once dominated the international system. The International Monetary Fund, the World Bank, the World Trade Organization, and NATO extended U.S. influence into every corner of international security and the global economy.

That's not true anymore. The so-called BRICS countries—China, India, Russia, Brazil, and South Africa—have established a developing-world club of their own. In 2014, the bloc announced plans to create a $100 billion development bank, enabling these countries to invest strategically in more places than ever. By itself, the BRICS bank has no power to undermine U.S. dominance of the global financial system. But add the China Development Bank, the Brazilian Development Bank (BNDES), and an expanding list of important regional lending institutions, and the world's borrowers are no longer quite so dependent on Western lenders, who provide loans in exchange for (often painful) political and economic concessions. In 2013, the World Bank disbursed $52.6 billion. Brazil's BNDES invested $88 billion that year, and its Chinese equivalent extended loans valued at $240 billion.[12] Here's another measure of America's reduced international influence: China is now the world's lead trading nation. In 2012, the last year for which credible statistics are available, the United States had larger trade volumes than China with 76 countries, while Communist China traded more than the United States with 124.[13]

In some ways, Americans seem unconcerned with their government's diminished international influence. A Pew Research poll conducted in December 2013 found that for the first time in the fifty years Pew has asked this question, a majority of U.S. respondents said the United States "should mind its own business internationally and let other countries get along the best they can on their own." Just 38 percent disagreed. That's a double-digit shift from the historical norm. A full 80 percent agreed that the United States should "not think so much in international terms but concentrate more on our own national problems." In any country that has genuinely competitive elections, no president can sustain an expensive, ambitious foreign policy without reliable public support. In America, that support is no longer there.[14]

No one has more partners, friends, and allies than America. China and Russia have only partners of convenience. But the U.S. government has undermined its ability to persuade allies to share international burdens. The wars in Iraq and Afghanistan, the prison at Guantánamo Bay, and drone strikes inside other countries have all made it harder for foreign leaders to persuade their citizens to support U.S. policy. U.S. spy agencies have made things even more difficult—and not just in Europe. It's harder for a U.S. president to criticize autocrats for spying on their own people while explaining to Germany's chancellor and Brazil's president why American spies are reading their e-mail and listening to their phone calls.[15]

. . . but America Itself Is Not in Decline

The good news for Americans is that while their country's foreign policy is in decline, America itself is not. Put the strength of its domestic economy in context. Its per capita income is more than seven times higher than China's.[16] It is the world's largest exporter of goods and services.[17] It's the largest exporter of food.[18] America is blessed with an entrepreneurial culture that celebrates not what has been accomplished but what's next. It has deep and efficient capital markets, the lifeblood of a dynamic economy, and no country has a greater capacity for technological innovation. Former national security adviser Thomas Donilon captured this point perfectly in a speech delivered in April 2014 at Kansas State University. "The largest eight technology companies in the world by market capitalization are based in the United States.* And when it comes to the next frontiers in extraordinary breakout technology, like 3-D manufacturing, artificial intelligence, nanotechnology, cloud computing, robotics, big data, and advanced material science, American

---

* The Chinese e-commerce firm Alibaba has since entered the top group.

entrepreneurs and companies are leading the way." More than 30 percent of all the money spent on research and development in 2014, some $465 billion, was spent in the United States.[19] That's a crucial source of future strength.

Nowhere is the American capacity for innovation more obvious than in energy production. Not so long ago, every U.S. presidential campaign speech included a reference to America's "dangerous dependence on foreign oil."[20] Not anymore. U.S. companies have reinvented the way hydrocarbon energy is produced, launching an energy revolution with lasting global implications. Hydraulic fracturing, better known as fracking, has opened access to liquid energy deposits locked inside once-impenetrable rock formations. Breakthroughs in horizontal drilling methods are making the technology much more profitable.

The result is an historic surge in domestic U.S. energy production and a sharp reduction in America's dependence on imported oil. Natural gas prices in the United States have fallen dramatically in recent years. These changes have only just begun. In 2014, the United States became the world's largest oil producer, and by 2019 the country could become almost entirely energy self-sufficient.[21]

This revolution didn't happen by accident. New ideas and technologies are the product of a U.S. oil industry continuously reenergized by intense competition, one in which privately owned companies have ample access to affordable financing and a legal system that ensures that government can't simply seize oil-rich land for exploitation in the "national interest." The United States will no longer depend so heavily on unstable regions and unreliable partners, particularly in the Middle East, for the energy needed to power its economy. U.S. policymakers might well allow for the export of some of these new reserves to help improve ties with important allies.

Here's another crucial advantage: Time is on America's side. The United States enjoys favorable demographics at a time when Europe, Japan, and China are all aging much more quickly. In 1980, the median age, the point that divides a population into two numerically equal halves, was 22.1 years in China, 30.1 in the United States, 32.6 in Japan, and 36.7 in Germany. By 2015, median ages had advanced to 36.8 in China, 37.8 in the United States, 46.5 in Germany, and 46.5 in Japan.[22] A UN study forecasts that by 2050 the median age will be 40.6 in the United States, 46.3 in China, 51.5 in Germany, and 53.4 in Japan. A larger percentage of Americans will be in the workforce, and a smaller percentage will be drawing pensions, than in any of its most important economic competitors.[23]

Americans must do a better job of preparing their children to meet the demands of a globalized marketplace. (More on that later in the book.) But higher education is a different story. Seventeen of the world's top twenty research universities are based in the United States.[24] That's why so many political and business leaders in other countries still send their children to the United States to earn an undergraduate or graduate degree. Elites aren't the only ones knocking on America's door. Immigrants come to America because they know that no other country offers better opportunities. In the process, they bolster our youth and strength. Elements of our immigration system need reform. As Donilon and others have pointed out, "40 percent of the people receiving advanced degrees in science, technology, engineering, and mathematics at American universities are foreign nationals with no legal way to stay here." Fix that problem, and America can build a truly global workforce.

These advantages should not obscure the fact that there is much that Americans can and should do to revitalize the country. But they provide a foundation that will allow Washington to restore America's international leadership . . . if that's what Americans want.

* * * * * * *

The next president will inherit a long list of complex domestic challenges—to help American companies create jobs, find common ground between liberals and conservatives on immigration policy, develop an education reform plan that meets the needs of a diverse population of students, thread the political needle on tax policy, craft an energy policy that can power the domestic economy and help relieve the energy dependence of our friends on our rivals, manage the country's debt, and try to bridge the divide between left and right. None of that will prevent the new president from pursuing a foreign policy that will strengthen the United States of America. He or she will have real options to consider.

Let's look at those options. First, there is the argument that a superpower foreign policy no longer makes sense. Go to YouTube and enter the phrase "Marine Corps Commercial: Toward the Sounds of Chaos." You'll be treated to a powerfully photographed, heart-pounding sixty-second television ad that begins with a group of U.S. marines sprinting in full body armor toward rising smoke on the horizon and the ominous sounds of confusion and fear. A deep voice intones, "There are a few who move toward the sounds of chaos. Ready to respond at a moment's notice. And when the time comes, they are the first to move toward the sounds of tyranny, injustice, and despair."

It's just a slickly produced TV commercial, a recruiting tool aimed at boys watching football, but it beautifully captures the superhero ideal that, some believe, too often guides our conversation about America's role in the world. Once we reach the victims of tyranny, injustice, and despair, what do we do with them? Once we've got the fire out, do we rebuild their homes? Rebuild their schools and hospitals? Rebuild their governments? Rebuild their countries? What should we do with the bad guys? How long would all that take and what would it cost? We're not the world's fire department.

An increasing number of Americans now tell pollsters that Washington should spend much less time on other people's problems and more on helping America realize its true promise. We've spent enough to rebuild Iraq and Afghanistan, they insist, and it's past time for these countries to stand on their own. No more responsibilities overseas that threaten our safety, solvency, and self-confidence. Let's invest in America, spend fewer tax dollars on badly designed foreign policy adventures, and speak to the world not from the moral mountaintop but through the power of a positive example. This point of view has much to recommend it.

Others insist that we can't simply retreat and expect the world's problems to leave us alone. There are certain things Americans can and should do to pursue and defend U.S. interests overseas. The central flaw in our current strategy, they insist, is that we have no real priorities, that we think we can afford to make up our foreign policy as we go, and that our plans are designed to meet the world's needs before our own. We need to stop wasting so many lives and so much money, they argue, in a foolish attempt to remake the world in our image. We need a foreign policy that's designed to make America safer and more prosperous, not to prepare other countries for democracy and rule of law. China's leaders aren't exporting Chinese values. They're promoting and protecting China's interests. Washington ought to do the same. There's a lot to be said for this argument as well.

Still others warn that in today's interconnected world, it's dangerously naïve to believe that America can ever really be safe in an unsafe world. We can't create jobs and grow our economy without a stable *global* economy. No nation can do more than the United

States to promote and protect this better world, and it is America's values, not its economic weight or military might, that we leave behind when the troops head home. Values that help others stand on their own. Washington, they argue, must get its financial house in order, invest in a stronger America, and pursue U.S. interests around the world. But it is shortsighted to believe that we can only build lasting strength at home by retreating from the world or by renouncing our faith in the power of democracy, freedom of speech, rule of law, and freedom from poverty and fear to create broadly shared peace and prosperity. This argument has merits too.

Americans have real options. The United States *can* play global policeman if it wants to. It can't patrol every street or take down every bad guy, but it could play the dominant role in shaping military and economic outcomes in every region of the world. It could promote, protect, and defend the values that Americans say they believe in. Or we could build an ambitious foreign policy designed to put America first, one that risks American lives and devotes our resources only toward plans that will make America more secure and more prosperous. Or we could mind our own business internationally, let other countries get along the best they can, and invest in rebuilding American strength from within.

Which is the right choice? What do Americans really want? There is no more important question facing America's would-be leaders.

CHAPTER 2

Incoherent America

(1990–2015)

We have not had a clear articulation of what American foreign
policy is basically since the end of the Cold War.
—Former senator Jim Webb (D-VA),
October 5, 2014

I t's good to be young. No doubt about that. But if you're under
the age of thirty, you aren't lucky enough to have witnessed the
euphoria of the Cold War's end. You didn't experience jubilant
disbelief at the sight of champagne-drinking Germans dancing
atop the Berlin Wall, the surge of pure joy across Europe, the
awakened hopes for a better life inside communist-bloc countries,
the sense of triumph in America, of limitless possibility, and the
thrill of "watching the world wake up from history."* In 1989 and

---

* This is a lyric from the song "Right Here, Right Now," performed by the band Jesus Jones,
which became a hit in Europe and America in 1990–91.

1990, things that could not happen happened all at once. And from this tidal wave of promise came the phrase "new world order."

Ironically, the first to use these words to describe post–Cold War possibilities was Soviet leader Mikhail Gorbachev, who told the UN General Assembly during a speech in December 1988 that "further world progress is now possible only through the search for a consensus of all mankind, in movement toward a new world order." He added that "the idea of democratizing the entire world order has become a powerful sociopolitical force."[1] Gorbachev's bold vision of disarmament and cooperation created pressure on newly elected President George H. W. Bush to respond, and Bush answered in the lead-up to the first Gulf War with a speech before a joint session of Congress on September 11, 1990:

> Out of these troubled times . . . a new world order can emerge. . . . A hundred generations have searched for this elusive path to peace, while a thousand wars raged across the span of human endeavor, and today that new world is struggling to be born. A world quite different from the one we've known. A world where the rule of law supplants the rule of the jungle. A world in which nations recognize the shared responsibility for freedom and justice.[2]

Today those words seem preposterously grandiose. But in the afterglow of the Cold War's end, as American and Soviet leaders stood shoulder to shoulder, many Americans dreamed of things that never were and asked: Why not? The quick defeat of Saddam Hussein five months later added to the elation. "By God, we've kicked the Vietnam syndrome once and for all," declared the president. "The specter of Vietnam has been buried forever in the desert sands of the Arabian Peninsula." The president's approval rating shot to 89 percent.

Bush and National Security Adviser Brent Scowcroft further defined the "new world order" for their 1998 book *A World Transformed*. The "premise [was] that the United States henceforth would be obligated to lead the world community to an unprecedented degree, as demonstrated by the Iraqi crisis, and that we should attempt to pursue our national interests, wherever possible, within a framework of concert with our friends and the international community."[3] This is a more modest vision than the one offered in 1990, but the emphasis on America's obligation to lead the world toward a brighter future remained. A deep U.S. recession, public appetite for change, the electoral impact of third-party wild card Ross Perot, and Bill Clinton's formidable political talents came together to end Bush's political career in November 1992. But they did not much dampen the optimism guiding America's role in the world.

Bill Clinton

Arkansas governor Bill Clinton did not offer himself to voters as a master geopolitical strategist. His knowledge of (and interest in) foreign policy was limited, and he knew well that if the American people had wanted a president with a sophisticated understanding of international politics, they would have reelected George H. W. Bush by a wide margin. The Cold War was over, and just as British voters eager for their government to rebuild and create jobs replaced war hero Winston Churchill with socialist Clement Attlee just weeks after the guns fell silent across Europe in 1945, so recession-weary Americans replaced a Cold Warrior and foreign policy specialist with a man who promised to "focus like a laser beam" on reviving the U.S. economy.* Clinton warned in his inaugural address that "we must invest more in our own people, in their jobs, in their future, and at the same time cut our massive debt. And we must do so in a world in which we must compete for every opportunity."

Before leaving office, Republican president George H. W. Bush and the Democratic leadership in Congress committed to a significant reduction in military spending. Democratic president Bill Clinton and the Republican congressional leadership after 1994 agreed to extend those cuts. The aim was to create a "peace dividend," savings made possible by the Cold War's end that could be used to meet domestic challenges, help eliminate federal budget deficits, and keep income taxes low.[4]

Yet despite his domestic focus, Clinton embraced an expansive post–Cold War view of American power. That's why he also argued during his inaugural address that "America must continue to lead the world we did so much to make. While America rebuilds at home, we will not shrink from the challenges, nor fail to seize the opportunities, of this new world." Invest at home *and* continue to lead the world. Why not? Any country that can play the decisive role in three great conflicts within a span of seventy-five years can surely do as it chooses.

It didn't take long for President Clinton, the first post–Cold War U.S. commander in chief, to bite off more than America could chew. First, there was the misadventure in Somalia, where a battle against hunger and anarchy became an intense firefight with local warlords and a humiliating setback for U.S. forces. In 1991, warring

---

* Churchill gained political revenge by winning a rematch and replacing Attlee as prime minister in 1951. The elder Bush gained his satisfaction only indirectly, when his son defeated Clinton's vice president, Al Gore, in 2000.

clans ousted Somali president Mohammed Siad Barre, and the ensuing civil war destroyed the country's agriculture and much of its food supply. The American engagement began when international media reported that more than three hundred thousand Somalis had died of starvation, and that armed militias led by local strongmen were stealing most of the international relief supplies and selling them abroad in exchange for weapons. President Bush responded in August 1992 with "Operation Provide Relief," sending U.S. troops to help distribute food and medicine to Somalis. The United States then led a multinational coalition that provided tons of food and medicine over the following weeks, but intensifying civil war among multiple militias continued to exacerbate a growing humanitarian disaster.

In December 1992, Operation Provide Relief became the much more ambitious "Operation Restore Hope," as the United States assumed command of a multinational military force with a UN mandate. A peace conference in March 1993 produced a ccase-fire agreement among Somalia's various warring factions, but it became clear within weeks that warlord Mohammed Farrah Aidid was using the break in fighting to strengthen his militia's position. Bloodshed resumed, and Aidid began to inflict casualties on coalition troops. President Clinton upped the ante on July 12 with a targeted airstrike meant to kill Aidid. The attack missed the strongman and killed dozens of Somali bystanders, swinging public sentiment in Mogadishu, the Somali capital, against U.S. troops. In the first days of October, the battle of Mogadishu, recreated in the book and film *Black Hawk Down,* killed eighteen Americans, one Pakistani, one Malaysian soldier fighting for the U.S.-led coalition, and hundreds of Somalis. Having sustained these losses in a fight that had no clear bearing on U.S. national security, Clinton ordered a phased withdrawal of U.S. troops.

In Somalia, the Clinton administration assumed that peace-keeping missions are much more likely to succeed where there is no effective local government to limit the freedom of action for international forces. Instead, Somalia's anarchy ensured that there was no local authority to give the operation local legitimacy. Clinton also failed to see that the force he dedicated to the task of bringing order to Somalia was not properly equipped for the job, and that U.S. public support for operations that are poorly understood will evaporate when things go badly wrong.

Nor did Clinton and those who advised him recognize that beyond the threat from local clan leaders was a challenge from terrorists, led by a still-embryonic al-Qaeda, which used skills acquired fighting the Soviets in Afghanistan to train Somalis to kill Americans. The assumptions that led the Clinton administration to believe that an improvised U.S.-led military operation could quickly bring order to an African state plagued by warlords and jihadis—and President Clinton's subsequent decision to retreat—may have emboldened al-Qaeda to launch the August 1998 attacks on U.S. embassies in Kenya and Tanzania that killed 234 people, including 12 Americans, and the suicide attack on the USS *Cole* that killed 17 U.S. sailors off Yemen in October 2000. These attacks then led to September 11, 2001. President Clinton committed the United States to a military engagement without understanding its enemies or their capabilities. The blowback continues.

The second example of President Clinton's poor foreign policy judgment grew directly from the Cold War's conclusion. Did the George H. W. Bush administration promise Soviet leader Mikhail Gorbachev that in exchange for Soviet support for the reunification of Germany in 1990, NATO would not expand "one inch" in Russia's direction?[5] If so, Washington broke that promise in 1999, when Bill Clinton supported NATO membership for former Soviet allies

Poland, Hungary, and the Czech Republic. It broke it again in 2004, when President George W. Bush backed admission for Romania, Bulgaria, Slovakia, Slovenia, and former Soviet republics Estonia, Latvia, and Lithuania. But the question of broken promises misses the point. Whatever the United States and its allies told Gorbachev in 1990, the expansion of NATO was a bad idea with predictably bad results. It expanded an alliance that no longer had a clear mandate, adding to the incoherence driving U.S. strategic thought.

It was a mistake to believe that post-Soviet Russia would understand Washington and its intentions in an entirely new way—or that America's postwar dominance would force it to. According to this rosy view of Russia, Ronald Reagan and Mikhail Gorbachev made crucial decisions in the Cold War's final days that allowed Bill Clinton's America and Boris Yeltsin's Russia to become fast friends and drinking buddies. The great post–Cold War challenge, Americans were told, was not in managing Moscow's strength but its weakness—its struggling economy, internal divisions, and search for a new identity. For a time that was true. In 1998, Yeltsin was powerless to stop the U.S. and European attempt to halt Yugoslavia's civil war with an assault on Serbia, a traditional Russian ally that the West denounced as an aggressor. To reassure Yeltsin, Clinton invited Russia to join the G7 group of industrialized democracies—as if America could slap Russia in the face on Monday and win it back with a hug on Tuesday. Nor could Yeltsin persuade Clinton to halt the first round of NATO expansion or Vladimir Putin persuade George W. Bush to halt the second. The United States and its allies pushed forward with NATO enlargement probably because they believed that though old Russian habits die hard, Moscow would surely recognize that the Cold War was over, that NATO posed no further threat to Russia, and that Moscow had little choice but to swallow this indignity.

Yet Russia would not remain weak forever, and many Russians did not share Yeltsin's tolerance for American triumphalism. When Putin was first elected president in 2000, Russia's per capita GDP stood at just $1,772, according to the World Bank. By 2013, that number had climbed to more than $14,600, largely thanks to the rise in oil prices over that period and the surge in state revenue it generated.[6] Putin's popularity rose too. By pushing full speed ahead with NATO expansion, Clinton (and George W. Bush) made it easy for Putin to persuade his people that Americans were rubbing Russian noses in Cold War defeat and that Russia needed a leader unafraid to face down further U.S. aggression. Putin's anti-Americanism remains a crucial source of his still-considerable popularity, and he used it to build a new Russian autocracy.[7]

There is a third important area in which President Clinton overestimated his ability to persuade another government to accept Washington's worldview. The forty-second president can be justifiably proud of two crucial accomplishments in America's all-important relations with China. He persuaded Congress to grant China "permanent normal trade relations," ending the politically toxic annual debate in Congress over U.S.-Chinese trade.[8] And he helped shepherd China toward membership in the World Trade Organization, which committed Beijing to lower tariffs on U.S.-made products, to open Chinese markets to U.S. services, and to comply with all WTO rules. These are real achievements. But Clinton justified his decision to pursue this strategy by arguing that increased trade would have a profound political impact inside China. "Just as democracy helps make the world safe for commerce," he argued in 1996, "commerce helps make the world safe for democracy. It's a two-way street."[9]

If Clinton hoped to open opportunities for U.S. (and other foreign) companies, he succeeded. That's important. But if he genuinely believed that greater economic openness would compel the Chinese Communist Party to play a less direct role in China's economy, that economic change would strengthen rule of law within the country, that China would offer greater protections for the human rights of its citizens as a result, that it would take a more cooperative attitude toward U.S. foreign policy and a less aggressive approach to its neighbors, or that it would move toward Western-style democracy, he miscalculated. He badly overestimated the power of economic change to empower China's people at the expense of their government. If he *didn't* really believe these things—if he was making this argument only to build support for the commercial aspects of the deal—he should have been more honest about China with the American people.

Candidate Bill Clinton seemed to understand that voters wanted Cold War victory to refocus Washington on domestic priorities. That's how "It's the economy, stupid" became one of the most famous campaign slogans in modern American history.[10] But Clinton stumbled into Somalia as if moral outrage and a genuine desire to end suffering were good enough reasons to send American soldiers into a conflict his administration should have known it didn't understand. He then stumbled out of Somalia in a way that emboldened terrorists to believe that a little effort and creative planning could force America into retreat more quickly and easily in 1993 than the Soviets were pushed from Afghanistan in 1989. He did not understand that a strengthened economy in Russia would allow a future Russian president, one far more popular than Boris Yeltsin, to use America's new world order to bolster his own domestic popularity and anti-Western credentials. Nor did Clinton see that opening China's economy would strengthen, not weaken, the country's authoritarian rule.

Despite his foreign policy failings, Bill Clinton presided over a remarkable run of prosperity. The U.S. economy created nearly twenty-three million new jobs during the eight years of his presidency. Unemployment fell from 7.3 percent to a historically remarkable 4.2 percent. The poverty rate dropped from 15.1 percent to 11.7 percent.[11] The shortsightedness of his foreign policy mistakes was not yet fully apparent as his presidency drew to a close, but the scandals that plagued his White House opened the door for change in 2000, and George W. Bush ran a disciplined and effective election campaign.

George W. Bush

On foreign policy, candidate Bush made a compelling case. "If we're an arrogant nation, they'll resent us; if we're a humble nation, but strong, they'll welcome us," he argued during a presidential debate in October 2000. "Our nation stands alone right now in the world in terms of power, and that's why we've got to be humble, and yet project strength in a way that promotes freedom."[12] He also asserted during that debate that "I don't think our troops ought to be used for what's called nation-building. I think our troops ought to be used to fight and win war."[13] On another occasion he declared himself "worried about an opponent who uses nation-building and the military in the same sentence."[14]

There is no reason to doubt that George W. Bush meant these things when he said them, and he could afford to make this (popular) argument, because there were no major conflicts visible on the horizon in 2000 that might draw in large numbers of U.S. ground troops. In the early days of his administration, the president was tested only by a diplomatic tangle over a collision involving U.S. and Chinese pilots and a politically charged decision over federal funding for stem cell research. But on September 11, 2001, another president hoping to focus his attention on winning support for tax cuts found himself flying through the eye of a Category 5 national security hurricane. To paraphrase a quote often attributed to Leon Trotsky, "You may not be interested in war, but war is interested in you." No one understands that better than George W. Bush.

After 9/11, the president committed the nation to an ill-defined, open-ended "global war on terror," a fight to subdue an enemy with no face. Money was no object. "Deficits don't matter," Vice President Dick Cheney famously asserted in 2002. Bill Clinton's failure to recognize the limits of American power was a product of post–Cold War euphoria. President George W. Bush's inability or unwillingness to accept U.S. limits grew from a conviction that the fear and righteous anger that followed the 9/11 attacks justified almost any expense of any kind in pursuit of justice and security.

The September 11 hijackers fundamentally altered American assumptions about the country's role in the world and its permanent vulnerability to threats hatching in the shadows of every unmonitored corner of the planet. The attacks persuaded some within the Bush administration that the time had come to use American power to give history a firm push in the direction of democracy. The result was a plan to rid the Middle East of those, like Iraq's Saddam Hussein, who defied American hegemony and to stage elections in Iraq that might inspire others across the region to demand democracy from their own leaders. Compounding the incoherence of this strategy, while diverting billions toward these transformational foreign policy projects, the Bush administration also pushed through tax cuts in 2001 and 2003 that totaled more than $1.6 trillion, and added an unfunded prescription drug benefit in December 2003 that cost the federal government more than $500 billion.[15] All this while fighting a global war and attempting to re-build two of the most unstable countries on earth.

The incoherence of the Bush years inflicted lasting damage on public attitudes toward the United States. Between 2000 and 2008, the Pew Research Center's Global Attitudes Project surveyed more than 175,000 people in fifty-four countries and the Palestinian territories on a variety of subjects. As noted in the report, published in December 2008, "these years coincide almost exactly with the presidency of George W. Bush, thus making it possible to assess his impact on matters of concern not just to the United States but to the world." The verdict? "America's image gap is the central, unmistakable finding from surveys conducted over the course of this decade."

In particular:

The U.S. image abroad is suffering almost everywhere. . . . Opposition to key elements of American foreign policy is widespread in Western Europe, and positive views of the U.S. have declined steeply among many of America's long-time European allies. In Muslim nations, the wars in Afghanistan and particularly Iraq have driven negative ratings nearly off the charts. The United States earns positive ratings in several Asian and Latin American nations, but usually by declining margins. And while the most recent Pew Global Attitudes survey finds that favorable views of America edged up in 2008, only in sub-Saharan Africa does America score uniformly favorable marks.[16]

When U.S. national security is directly at stake, the president has a responsibility to act, with or without the support of other governments. But the attitudes reflected in these polls matter, because when a country's citizens hold a dim view of America and its foreign policy, it becomes more difficult for that country's leaders to back Washington on anything that might generate controversy. In an interconnected and dangerous world where the power gap between the United States and emerging powers is narrowing, Washington needs friends and partners.

Yet greater than the damage to America's image abroad was the sense of defeatism and frustration created at home by a foreign policy driven by superhero hubris. With U.S. troops bogged down on the ground in Iraq and Afghanistan, the elder President Bush's claim to have buried the "Vietnam syndrome" echoed like a boast from an era of foolish innocence. The younger President Bush helped improve U.S. relations with both China and India, noteworthy accomplishments, particularly as China's surging economy and rising commodity prices lifted the economies of emerging powers like India, Brazil, Russia, Turkey, Mexico, South Korea, South Africa, and others to new heights. Bush also deepened U.S. ties with governments in sub-Saharan Africa, home to the world's fastest-growing middle class, as no U.S. president has ever done.

Yet the long, costly, frustrating wars in Iraq and Afghanistan led the president to become the most ambitious nation-builder in U.S. history. In July 2014, the Special Inspector General for Afghanistan Reconstruction issued a quarterly report addressed to Congress. Among other things, it found that "by the end of 2014, the United States will have committed more funds to reconstruct Afghanistan, in inflation-adjusted terms, than it spent on 16 European countries after World War II under the Marshall Plan." At least Americans understood why postwar Western Europe was worth rebuilding.[17] Exhausted by costly commitments that seemed to have no end, Americans then found themselves trapped inside the worst financial crisis since the Great Depression, and millions of American voters decided in November 2008 that the time had come to elect a true newcomer, a smiling face unblemished by the ugly choices and bad decisions of the previous decade. Just as American voters weary of Vietnam and Watergate elected a friendly, engaging Georgia peanut farmer to lead the nation in 1976, so the electorate turned in 2008 toward a charismatic junior senator from Illinois, the first African-American candidate to win a major party's nomination for president. For many Americans, election night brought catharsis. For his supporters, national renewal seemed finally at hand.

Barack Obama

By the time Barack Obama took the oath of office in January 2009, the sense of superpower opportunity and limitless possibility was long gone. The new president inherited a financial sector in free fall, two wars that few Americans continued to support, and high expectations for a new beginning in Washington. Obama's foreign policy goals were modest, not simply because, like Bill Clinton and George W. Bush, his interest and expertise were focused primarily on domestic policy, but also because American power was overextended and everybody knew it. His immediate priorities? First, do no harm. Lead a multinational effort to stabilize the global economy. Revitalize America's economy. End wars. Don't start new ones.

Beyond this, Obama turned to former presidential rival Hillary Clinton, who became his secretary of state, to lead a shift in the country's long-term foreign policy priorities. The result was the "pivot to Asia," a redirection of presidential attention, commercial ambition, and military assets toward East Asia. There were many reasons for this shift. China is the world's most important rising power, and America's relationship with that country will help determine how peaceful and prosperous the world will be over the next half century. India is another emerging power with enormous potential as a political, trade, and investment partner. Japan, a traditional U.S. ally, remains the world's third-largest economy and an increasingly important player in East Asia's security. Rising powers like South Korea and Indonesia, and promising upstarts like the Philippines and Vietnam, add to the region's importance. North Korea remains the world's least predictable nuclear-armed wild card, and East Asia lacks the kind of regional institutions that help keep the peace in Europe. America and the world have a lot at stake there.

But President Obama saw not only risk in Asia but an important opportunity. China's rise as an economic and military power continues to generate deep anxiety among its neighbors, creating demand in those countries for better relations with the United States to avoid too deep a dependence on the sturdiness of China's economy and the goodwill of its government. Obama appeared ready to grab this chance to broaden and deepen trade ties with the region's dynamic economies and to establish a security foothold to help mitigate the risk of regional conflict. The greater U.S. regional presence could also help improve ties with Beijing if the Obama administration could persuade China's leaders that the United States intended to deepen mutually lucrative trade and investment ties with China and act as an honest broker to help keep East Asia peaceful during a delicate moment in China's development.

By choosing as their primary foreign policy tool "economic statecraft" rather than military pressure, the new president and his ambitious secretary of state also appeared to have learned something from the overreach of their immediate predecessors. This is how Secretary Clinton defined the new strategy in 2012: "We [are] updating our foreign policy priorities to take economics more into account . . . turning to economic solutions for strategic challenges . . . stepping up commercial diplomacy—what I like to call jobs diplomacy—to boost U.S. exports, open new markets, and level the playing field for our businesses. . . . In short, we are shaping our foreign policy to account for both the economics of power and the power of economics."[18]

It's not that President Obama swore off all use of military power. By approving a "troop surge" in Afghanistan in 2009, moving on Libya's Muammar Qaddafi in 2011, and ordering airstrikes on the terrorist juggernaut ISIS in Iraq and Syria in 2014, Obama proved he would authorize military force to answer particular challenges. But this president recognized that even the commander in chief of the world's only military superpower has limited ability to use force to get what he wants. Nor did Obama intend to ignore the world outside East Asia. Efforts to repair damaged relationships with European allies, reach a negotiated settlement to prevent Iran from developing nuclear weapons, and reshape international perceptions of the United States all remained important goals.

But though Obama began with a coherent foreign policy strategy, intense battles at home over health care reform and the federal budget and his lack of interest in foreign policy allowed him to become easily distracted. The eruption of the Arab Spring in 2011 caught the White House flat-footed. Eventual support for pro-democracy demonstrators across the region alienated Saudi Arabia, America's primary authoritarian friend in the Middle East. Civil war in Syria drew the president in deeply enough to put his credibility on the line but not enough to decide the conflict's outcome. The president threatened "enormous consequences" if Syria's Bashar al-Assad used chemical weapons on his country's battlefields.[19]

Assad then used these weapons, and when Obama found little international support for a U.S. strike on Assad, he settled for a Russian-brokered agreement that required the Syrian president to destroy his remaining weapons. A crisis in Ukraine drew the president into a confrontation with Russia that brought real economic risk with little potential reward beyond satisfaction in defending a principle. A plan to negotiate a lasting political settlement between Israelis and Palestinians ground to a halt in early 2014, squandering more U.S. credibility. Weeks later, a volcanic eruption of violence between Israel and Hamas killed more than two thousand people in Gaza, the clear majority of them Palestinian civilians.[20]

Another problem: To win and maintain public support for his foreign policy, Obama has repeatedly made clear in advance the extent of America's commitment to meeting particular challenges. In the process, he has defined his foreign policy goals in negative terms—we won't put troops on the ground, we won't stay past December, we won't commit resources beyond our means, we won't move forward without partners—more often than any U.S. president in the past seventy-five years. For some Americans, that's a welcome relief. Self-imposed limits are sensible when resources are limited. But announcing them in advance makes America's job tougher.

President Obama did not share his predecessors' illusions about the use of American power, but as I'll argue in a later chapter, his lack of a coherent worldview dissolved his commitment to the well-made plans of his first term, leaving him to improvise responses to events far beyond his (or anyone else's) control. Success for the pivot to Asia depends on the president's direct engagement in building the relationships that can do more than any other to enhance American security and prosperity over the coming generation. Instead, Obama finds himself in a series of international conflicts that impose high costs and risks for uncertain gains.

The president has added to the problem by confusing allies, enemies, and the American people about his administration's true intentions. Does Obama believe, as his rhetoric often implies, that America must lead in a dangerous world? Does he believe, as his actions often suggest, that America must choose much more carefully than in the past where it will lead and where it will not? Or does Obama believe that America must step back, allow space for others to lead, rebuild the country's strength from within, and reconsider Washington's most basic foreign policy assumptions?

Every plan is a good one until the first shot is fired, warned master military strategist Carl von Clausewitz.[21] Barack Obama is not the first American president to see his well-made plans overtaken by events, and he won't be the last. But President Obama has refused to choose a clear path forward. This is his great foreign policy failure. Candidate Obama, like candidate Clinton, promised to focus on rebuilding strength at home. Candidate Obama, like candidate Bush, warned that nation-building was beyond America's means. But President Obama refused to commit to any foreign policy framework to help him make difficult decisions. His priorities have shifted with changing headlines, he has drawn red lines to no effect, and the few commitments he has made have encouraged others to set tests of American will that the White House had no intention of passing.

* * * * * * *

No one believes anymore that superpower America bestrides the narrow world like a colossus, that America's threats are always heeded and its promises always kept. Our power and money are finite resources, and the world is fast becoming a more complicated and dangerous place. The number of foreign governments able to ignore our wishes and warnings will only grow in coming years. The costs of a quarter century of incoherent foreign policy continue to rise. And the American people continue to elect candidates who promise to focus on domestic goals.

Each time an international emergency arises, someone wants to know what America's president means to do about it. Sometimes we charge in on horseback. Sometimes we enter on tiptoe. Sometimes we do nothing and hope the problem will solve itself. But the sun has set on the day when America's president can do big things overseas without support from the American people. That support, lasting support, can only come from a frank appraisal of the costs, risks, and potential rewards at stake—and a firm decision about what role America can and should play in the world.

A quarter century has passed since the Berlin Wall came crashing down. Many more countries now have seats at the important tables. Hundreds of millions more people have entered the global middle class. Democracy has expanded, but so has conflict. In this world in transition, fires burn hotter and longer than before because it's no longer clear who can and will put them out. Hopes and fears now rise together—in America and around the world.

The incoherence in American foreign policy has been growing for twenty-five years. What are we going to do about it?

CHAPTER 3

Independent America
So That Security and Liberty May Prosper Together

Democracy is something we must always be working at. It is a
process never finished, never ending.
— Edmund de S. Brunner

"Every gun that is made, every warship launched, every rocket fired signifies, in the final sense, a theft from those who hunger and are not fed, those who are cold and are not clothed. This world in arms is not spending money alone. It is spending the sweat of its laborers, the genius of its scientists, the hopes of its children. The cost of one modern heavy bomber is this: a modern brick school in more than thirty cities. It is two electric power plants, each serving a town of sixty thousand population. It is two fine, fully equipped hospitals. It is some fifty miles of concrete pavement. We pay for a single fighter with a half million bushels of wheat. We pay

— 47 —

for a single destroyer with new homes that could have housed more than eight thousand people. This is not a way of life at all, in any true sense. Under the cloud of threatening war, it is humanity hanging from a cross of iron."

President Dwight Eisenhower delivered these words to the American Society of Newspaper Editors at the Statler Hotel in Washington on April 16, 1953. It was the new president's first formal address to the American people after just twelve weeks in office, and he titled it "Chance for Peace."* In his more famous farewell address delivered eight years later, Eisenhower warned of the rise of a "military-industrial complex," a "permanent arms industry of vast proportions" and its "unwarranted influence" in America's corridors of power. These two speeches frame the presidency of a man who first commanded public attention as one of the U.S. Army's most celebrated generals.

"Chance for Peace" was delivered at a critical historical moment. Joseph Stalin had been dead six weeks, and hopes for a less belligerent Soviet leadership were on the rise. The Korean War was grinding toward final stalemate. The United States announced the world's first hydrogen bomb in January; the Soviets unveiled one of their own in August. The Soviets sent soldiers into East Berlin to crush a workers' uprising in June. The U.S. Central Intelligence Agency engineered a coup to remove Iran's prime minister, Mohammad Mossadegh, in August, and Vice President Richard Nixon's visit to Tehran in December provoked days of deadly riots on Iranian streets. By expressing the cost of weapons in schools, homes, and hospitals, Eisenhower called on the Kremlin's new masters to abandon the forced march toward armed competition that he

---

* You can hear the entire speech on YouTube: http://www.youtube.com/watch?v=nz Nbfa1QyYg.

feared would bankrupt both countries. He urged Soviet leaders to see that the Cold War and its terrible costs were not inevitable.

More than six decades later, there is no Cold War, no determined superpower enemy with friends in every region, no nuclear arms race, and no credible foreign threat to America's survival. The risk of conflict with emerging China is limited by a deep economic interdependence with the United States that could never have existed between America and its Cold War communist rivals. Today's Russia would love to check American power, but it lacks the Soviet Union's ideological appeal, potent allies, and military reach. No coalition of would-be American adversaries measures up. Yet the United States continues to spend more on its military than all its potential competitors combined.[1] It's only natural that with so much money spent on advanced weapons, policymakers will find uses for them to justify the expense—and to be sure they perform as advertised—in ways that add to our debt, implicate us in crises that are none of our business, and further compromise our own security. Making matters worse, the 9/11 terror attacks have given birth to an enormous new security bureaucracy, one that deprives Americans of our privacy and inflicts lasting damage on relations with our allies.

For all these reasons, Ike's message has never been more timely: "Only an alert and knowledgeable citizenry," he warned, "can compel the proper meshing of the huge industrial and military machinery of defense with our peaceful methods and goals so that security and liberty may prosper together."[2] That's an ideal worthy of an exceptional nation.

President Eisenhower also understood that debt cripples a nation's long-term strength, and that a balanced budget provides crucial support for both a dynamic economy and a strong military. During his final year in office, at the height of the Cold War, the

U.S. government posted a more than $1 billion *surplus*. In 2013, the federal deficit topped $680 billion, down from $1.1 trillion in 2012. By the end of 2015, the U.S. national debt surpassed $19 trillion.[3] For perspective, in 1960, the national debt was about 52 percent of the country's gross domestic product. By 1970, that figure had fallen to 34 percent. On October 17, 2013, it passed the 100 percent mark. In other words, the national debt now exceeds the value of America's entire economic output. There are many ways to measure America's indebtedness, and the sources of this slow-motion catastrophe extend well beyond defense spending, but we can't afford to ignore the fact that in the decade after 9/11, government spending on security and the military grew by nearly 120 percent. Both presidents and lawmakers, Democrats and Republicans, have contributed to this growing problem.

As the next wave of would-be American presidents takes to the campaign trail and debate stage, listen carefully to what they say about America's role in the world. Beware those who talk of responsibilities but never of price tags. Measure the costs of their foreign policy promises in American schools, homes, and hospitals—and in money that might have stayed in the taxpayer's pocket. Reject those who claim that America can afford to police the world.

It's time for a new declaration of independence—a proclamation of emancipation from the responsibility to solve everyone else's problems. Americans deserve a government dedicated to the proposition that security and liberty may prosper together. We can no longer accept burdens abroad that undermine our values at home, sap our strength and resources, entangle us in fights that are not our concern, and threaten the heart of our democracy. This independent spirit is not selfish. It is neither cowardly nor defeatist. It is the foundation upon which Americans will build a

prosperous and secure nation that can inspire the world to follow
its example.

Overreach

It's a tough job being the world's policeman. A U.S. president who
considers himself "leader of the free world" must worry over a very
long list of other people's headaches. Which of its former Soviet
neighbors is Russia bullying this week? When will North Korea
test-fire another missile? Is it America's responsibility to ensure that
Israelis and Palestinians sign a deal that neither side appears to
want, or that China and Japan reach some agreement about who
did what to whom in 1937? Must we intervene to ensure they don't
come to blows over a pile of contested rocks in the East China Sea?
Yes, history matters, but that's their history, not ours.

Is Venezuela selling weapons to Colombian rebels? Are Somali
pirates attacking cargo ships in the Indian Ocean? Is Kandahar
secure? Is Kashmir quiet? Are jihadis on the move in Mali? Is a
despot in Syria about to slaughter large numbers of his own people?
Something must be done, but if we accept the moral responsibility
to do something about those things, aren't we then bound to ensure
that local strongmen aren't doing the same in Sudan, Sierra Leone,
and the Central African Republic? Or nuclear-armed North Korea? What would that responsibility cost? On what moral basis
must we choose which of these burdens to accept and which to ignore? Pity the poor American taxpayer.

Not that our allies are ever satisfied with America's help. Consider this passage from a memoir by former defense secretary Robert Gates on a conversation about Iran with the Saudi king:

[Saudi king] Abdullah . . . wanted a full-scale military attack on Iranian military targets, not just the nuclear sites. He warned that if we did not attack, the Saudis "must go our own way to protect our interests." . . . He was asking the United States to send its sons and daughters into a war with Iran in order to protect the Saudi position in the Gulf and the region. . . . He was asking us to shed American blood, but at no time did he suggest that any Saudi blood might be spilled. He went on and on about how the United States was seen as weak by governments in the region. The longer he talked, the angrier I got.[4]

In fiscal year 2012, the American taxpayer provided 186 countries with a total of $42 billion.[5] Many of the governments that receive this help want Washington to guarantee their security—even as they pursue their own agendas. Pakistan received $834 million in economic help and $361 million for its security services for fiscal year 2013, two years after Osama bin Laden was found hiding in a compound within easy walking distance of Pakistan's most prestigious military academy.[6] Since 2002, the United States has provided Afghanistan with more than $100 billion in financial aid. The American taxpayer will never know exactly how many of the schools and government buildings constructed with their money have survived—and how much of the money has simply been stolen. Imagine what $100 billion might have built at home.

Becoming Superman

How did we come to accept all these burdens? It was war that lifted the United States to superpower status and cast us in the role of international policeman—a responsibility that some in the United States remain all too eager to accept. The twentieth century's two world wars elevated America, diminished our allies, and (temporarily) subdued potential rivals like the Soviet Union and China. Neither war was ever fought in an American city. Certainly, U.S. soldiers and their families paid dearly for both victories, but when the doughboys of the American Expeditionary Forces arrived in France in June 1917, World War I had already raged across Europe for nearly three years. About 116,000 Americans were killed during the Great War. Compare that with more than 1.7 million Germans, 1.7 million Russians, nearly 1.4 million French, about 1.2 million from Austria-Hungary, and more than 900,000 Britons.[7] The war's economic and psychological impact on these countries was without precedent.

A generation later, it took a "sudden and deliberate" Japanese attack on Pearl Harbor to bring America into World War II, and though the war in the Pacific began soon after, Americans didn't arrive on the beaches of Normandy until nearly five years after Hitler's invasion of Poland. American families made profound and permanent sacrifices for victory in World War II, but compare 418,000 Americans killed with the deaths of more than 20 million Soviets, 7 million Germans, and perhaps 3 million Japanese.

Then there was the economic toll. World War II cut Europe's agricultural output by half and its industrial production by two-thirds. It leveled about 40 percent of buildings in Germany's fifty largest cities.[8] It cost Japan's emperor more than 80 percent of his Asian territory. Many of Japan's largest cities were left virtually uninhabitable.[9] The war cost France 20 percent of its houses, half its livestock, two-thirds of its railways, and about 45 percent of its total national wealth.[10] It destroyed seventy thousand Soviet towns and villages.[11] Britain's trade was cut to 30 percent of prewar levels, and the sun finally began to set on the British Empire.[12] Impoverished China moved from Japanese occupation to civil war.

In America, on the other hand, after a dozen years of economic depression, the war created seventeen million new jobs to meet sky-rocketing demand for weapons and materiel. American salaries doubled during the war, and savings accounts increased sevenfold.[13] The U.S. standard of living surged, and unemployment virtually disappeared. By prudently resisting the call to arms for as long as possible, the United States became the world's most powerful country, one that sometimes appears to believe that its destiny is to save the world from itself.

Despite Eisenhower's warning, the United States then donned Superman's cape. Gone were the days when Washington treated war as a last resort. Since the dawn of the Cold War, every U.S. president and the leaderships of both parties in Congress have led their country into conflict after conflict in the name of remaking the world in America's image, allegedly to make us more secure at home. Did the war in Korea make us safer or more prosperous? What lesson did we learn in Vietnam? Forty years after the fall of Saigon, there is still no consensus answer to this question. Forget the brief military adventures in Grenada and Panama. Most Americans already have.

The end of the Cold War did not diminish the American appetite for a fight. Did the liberation of Kuwait put an end to Washington's conflict with Saddam Hussein? Americans have spent hundreds of billions of dollars in Afghanistan. How did it become America's longest war,* and what did American efforts there ac-

---

* The war in Afghanistan lasted thirteen years and two months. Vietnam lasted ten years and two months. Iraq extended eight years and nine months. U.S. troops fought in World War II for three years and eight months. Both the Korean War and the Philippine-American War lasted three years and one month. The United States fought in World War I for just one year and seven months.

complish? The second war with Iraq cost hundreds of billions more. Is that country more secure today than it was in 2002? Have support for dictators, the ouster of leaders like Iran's Mossadegh, Congo's Patrice Lumumba, and Chile's Salvador Allende, the Guantánamo Bay prison, the sorry spectacle at Abu Ghraib, torture, rendition, cyber-conflict, drones, and the sale of weapons to the enemies of America's enemies made the United States stronger, safer, and more prosperous? Even if you believe they have, these kinds of policies are not sustainable in a world that debt-laden America no longer dominates.

Sometimes Washington's attempt to impose its will produces the opposite of its intended result. In his 2002 State of the Union address, President George W. Bush identified an "axis of evil" consisting of North Korea, Iraq, and Iran. Bush administration officials warned that Iran was increasingly dangerous. But if the war on Saddam Hussein was intended in part as a message to Iran that it must give up its nuclear program or risk a U.S. invasion, it didn't work. Instead, Iran's leaders, who suddenly found themselves encircled by American troops in Afghanistan to the east and Iraq to the west, came to a different conclusion. The United States had not invaded North Korea, they could safely assume, precisely because the North Koreans already had nuclear weapons. The United States could afford to invade Iraq, Iranians reasoned, because it didn't have nuclear weapons. The best way to prevent a U.S. invasion, therefore, was to develop a nuclear weapon as quickly as possible while Superman remained busy in Iraq and Afghanistan. Thus the money and lives lost in ousting Saddam only strengthened Iran's determination to build a bomb.

The U.S. taxpayer hasn't gotten better value for the money under President Obama, who has presided over a substantial expansion of the U.S. intelligence community begun under President

Bush. During the Eisenhower years, military spending represented a higher percentage of U.S. GDP than it does today, but that was at an early Cold War moment before Social Security, Medicare, Medicaid, and other social safety net spending represented more than half of U.S. federal spending.[14] And it was easier to understand the growth of the military-industrial complex at a time when two military superpowers were playing out a zero-sum competition for power and influence in every corner of the world. Today, America's intelligence agencies are spying not only on potential threats to U.S. national security, but on the leaders of friendly countries like Germany and Brazil. Worse, evidence has emerged that the National Security Agency may have spied on members of the U.S. Congress. Why would the NSA do this? Perhaps merely because it can. Something has to change.

The Hidden Cost of War

When it comes to America's wars, the price tags we know about are bad enough. Today, many of those costs, human and material, are hidden, making it all the more difficult for an "alert and knowledgeable citizenry" to ensure that Americans understand and endorse the actions that their government takes on their behalf and with their money. First, there was the end of selective service. Few Americans miss the chaotic confrontations of the 1960s, when policemen in battle formation faced off on city streets and college campuses with angry young Americans, many of whom feared they might be drafted and sent to fight in Vietnam. Few want a return of the draft, but when Richard Nixon abolished it in 1973, he took an important step toward hiding the true cost of war from average Americans.

That process continues today as hundreds of billions of dollars are spent each year to widen the U.S. military's technological advantage over potential rivals and to make wars look less like bloody confrontations and more like video games. In particular, the use of drone aircraft further desensitizes Americans to their impact on the rest of the world by providing a lower-cost method of killing people that puts fewer U.S. soldiers in harm's way. Unfortunately, some of the people killed by drones—we'll never know exactly how many—are guilty mainly of being in the wrong place at the wrong time, including inside countries like Pakistan and Yemen with which the United States is not at war. Do Americans understand that? Are they aware what the rest of the world thinks of this practice?[15] Do they care?

When it comes to hiding costs, it's one thing to lower taxes during wartime, as President George W. Bush did in the early days of his global war on terror. But the use of drones takes this cynical logic to an ugly extreme—and they create new enemies for Washington to track. Drone strikes inside Pakistan and Yemen can never really make us immune to terrorist attacks inside the United States. Our actions in the Middle East and South Asia make us *more* vulnerable at home, by persuading a new generation of Pakistanis, Yemenis, and others that it's better to attack Americans who aren't wearing state-of-the-art body armor and flying robot aircraft. The end of the draft and the use of drones make it easier for presidents to pretend that Americans can have what they want without paying for it. And that makes America's leaders much less accountable on the most important decisions that voters empower them to make.

Just as some want technology to do the dirty work, others say we can simply lean more heavily on our friends and allies. It worked in Libya, where U.S. financial and logistical support helped French and British pilots take down perennial headache Muammar Qaddafi. Isn't that a possible model that might allow the United States to achieve more of its foreign policy goals at less cost and risk? Can't the United States do a little more "leading from behind"? But Libya was an exceptional case. Qaddafi is that rare leader who had virtually no powerful friends outside his country, and the invitation to stop him came directly from other Arab governments—an extraordinarily uncommon event. More to the point, the end of Qaddafi has done little for the United States and has yet to bring peace for the Libyan people. Much more common is the case of Syria, where toppling a tyrant depends on the willingness of outsiders to send in ground troops. Neither Washington nor its European allies proved foolish enough to commit to another costly and potentially intractable war in the Middle East—coalition or no.

NATO Is Not the Answer

Yet the dream that Superman can simply ask his "Super Friends" for help will not go away, and Russia's shift toward a more hostile approach to the West encourages the hope that NATO might finally find a post–Cold War mission. Is NATO prepared to fight for Ukraine? It's satisfying to imagine an embarrassing loss for a Russian regime that appears to think its ability to manipulate its smaller neighbor provides evidence of its timeless greatness. Everyone likes watching a bully take one in the teeth.

Take a closer look. This is no simple morality tale, and a deeper understanding of Ukraine's largely self-inflicted predicament tells an important story about the foolishness of our current foreign policy. Americans believe in self-determination. They believe that no country is simply another's satellite, that empires are inherently immoral, that Ukraine should be allowed to decide for itself which clubs to join, and that Russians deserve no veto on this matter. But Ukraine's central problem is that the corruption that plagued both its pro-Russian and pro-European governments has robbed that country of its ability to pay its bills. No revolution can solve that mundane problem.

Though a clear majority of its citizens are ethnic Ukrainians, more than seven million Russian-speaking ethnic Russians still live within Ukraine's borders. In some cases, their families have occupied that land for decades or longer. We don't understand the history, and it's none of our business. What if Russia one day decides to make military mischief in Latvia or Estonia? These are former Soviet republics with larger Russian minorities than Ukraine has. In both these smaller countries, ethnic Russians make up more than a quarter of the population. Unlike Ukraine, those countries are NATO members. If Russia attacks, Article 5 of the North Atlantic Treaty will obligate the United States to treat an armed attack on Latvia as an invasion of Louisiana. How much public support can any U.S. president expect if he is one day forced to honor that pledge?

In March 2014, YouGov asked one thousand adult Americans if the United States should use military force if Russia attacks one of its neighbors. Just 40 percent said the United States should defend Poland, 29 percent would support a defense of Turkey, and just 21 percent would support a U.S. defense of Latvia. All three are NATO members. Only 56 percent of those surveyed would defend Britain.[16] If you can harely get a majority of Americans to support a defense of Britain, it's clear that the American people want no more foreign wars of choice.

NATO was crucial for Cold War success. But the Cold War is over. Russia is not our friend, but it is hardly a formidable superpower enemy, and America can no longer afford to bankroll so much of NATO's operations. Lord Ismay, NATO's first secretary-general, famously said in 1949 that NATO's purpose was "to keep the Russians out, the Americans in, and the Germans down." Sixty-six years later, it's unclear whether most Europeans still want the Americans in, but it is perfectly clear that the Germans are no longer down. Unless Europeans (particularly Germans) are willing to pick up a larger share of the tab for NATO operations, why should American taxpayers pour in billions of dollars more? Why should Americans lead a fight to defend Latvia or Estonia if Germany, now one of the world's wealthiest nations, won't share more of the cost?

No More Nation-Building

Some say that terrorism is the greatest threat to America's national security and that Superman must maintain an aggressive, "forward-leaning" global presence to destroy terrorists in their nests rather than try to find and stop them only after they have entered our country. We fight the terrorists "over there"—in Iraq, Afghanistan, Yemen, Somalia, and elsewhere—so that we don't have to fight them at home, and we invest billions to rebuild countries like Iraq and Afghanistan, states that we have dismantled, in order to deny terrorists the ungoverned expanses of territory they need in order to live, plan, train, and launch attacks.

Unfortunately, as we've learned in recent years, the United States isn't very good at building open democratic societies in hostile faraway places, and the expense is not worth the effort even if it were—not with urgent needs at home. We have more than enough power to destroy states, but we don't have the resources we need, including U.S. public support, to rebuild them. U.S. withdrawal, always a mere matter of time, leaves vacuums of power in its wake, no matter how much we've spent to create the illusion of change. Terrorists know that recapturing safe havens is simply a matter of waiting us out or of moving across the border toward the next target of opportunity.

Are Afghanistan and Pakistan now free of Islamic militants? In Iraq and Syria, jihadis have built the best-funded terrorist group in the history of the world. If President Obama had been foolish enough to take down Bashar al-Assad and the Syrian military, who would rejoice? Those who see Syria as the next Turkey, a modern, moderate Muslim country? Or those who see it as the next Iraq, an inherently unstable sectarian battleground?

In countries without terrorists and where American interests are not under direct threat, our continuing presence is especially hard to understand. A quarter century after the end of the Cold War and seven decades after the end of World War II, there are still forty thousand U.S. troops stationed in Germany and fifty thousand more in Japan.[17] It's time for Europe and Japan to finally accept responsibility for their own security, to spend more money and risk more lives in their own defense. That is a role these wealthy countries should already have taken. Senior officials in Germany and Japan have admitted as much in recent years, and Washington should encourage them to spend the money and follow through.

Great Expectations

Americans imagine a world in which every country will one day embrace democracy. We know that some will take a long and winding road to get there. But in the end, we believe that "people power" will eventually trump tyranny. We assume that elections will replace bad guys with good guys, and that newly elected leaders will have to satisfy public demand for better government. Democracy, however, is a complex, long-term project. No country, not even the United States of America, has perfected it. And not even the United States has the staying power to ensure that the seeds it plants in foreign soil will one day take root—that they won't be scattered by the first strong wind. Americans don't understand the forces that block change and drive conflict in these countries, and the taxpayer can't afford to keep boots on the ground long enough for America's leaders to figure these things out.

Yet despite our recent setbacks, current U.S. foreign policy continues to represent the triumph of hope over experience, in part because there remains a messianic strain in America's approach to the world. It existed long before April 1917, when President Woodrow Wilson spoke of the German Empire's "reckless lack of compassion or of principle" and the resulting need to "make the world safe for democracy." Whether it is Democrats ready to fight for universal human rights that we will never have the power to enforce or hawkish Republicans who want to defeat evil wherever it's now making headlines, this fanaticism is alive and well. The long wars in Iraq and Afghanistan have sent this grandiosity into hibernation, but like General Douglas MacArthur, it shall return. One day soon, shortsighted leaders in both parties will push us into new commitments that we don't understand and can't afford to sustain.

It's not simply that we can't police the world. It's that we have no right to force those who disagree with us to see things our way. Americans like to believe that our country is so clearly a source of virtue that the rest of the world will invite us to bring about positive change in their lives. We believe that democracy is undeniably attractive and our commitment to it so obvious that others should simply trust us to create it for them within the borders of their countries.

We fail to see our double standards, but the world does not. The world sees that we criticize the conduct of elections in Russia and Venezuela—and that we laud every hollow "democratic reform" in Egypt or Saudi Arabia. We endorse the results of Israeli elections and condemn the outcome when Palestinians vote. We support self-determination for Kosovo but not Crimea. We tell Europeans which countries we think they should admit to the European Union. It's easier to tell others what to do when the gap between your power and theirs is large, but that gap has narrowed. It will narrow further still.[18]

We accuse China, Russia, and France of cyber-espionage even as Americans spy on pretty much everyone else—including other Americans. How can we champion "rule of law" when we refuse to abide by international rules or submit to the collective judgment of others? We cheer when some anti-American autocrat faces justice before the International Criminal Court, but the U.S. Senate will not ratify an agreement that might submit an American citizen to its jurisdiction.[19] How should we expect the rest of the world to respond to this double standard? We ignore the reality that others love their countries too, and that they don't consider themselves to be "Americans at an earlier stage of development." It is foolish and arrogant to believe that we know better than the citizens of other countries how their governments should spend, save, invest, and make laws.

Another flaw in our foreign policy: We love villains. Americans seem incapable of simply ignoring a foreign leader who shakes his fist at us, whether to make a name for himself at home or to express a legitimate grievance. And we make little effort to understand why his anti-Americanism makes him popular. It was easy to dismiss the late Hugo Chávez, Venezuela's bombastic former president, as a narcissistic clown. There is ample evidence that he and his successor have inflicted lasting damage on Venezuela and its economy. We don't have to trade with Venezuela—though we will surely continue to buy large amounts of its crude oil. We don't have to offer its leaders anything of value. But if we refuse to try to understand Chávez's appeal for the people who elected him, more than once and by significant margins,[20] we will never understand Venezuela or any other country in which anti-Americanism can boost the career of an aspiring politician. If we don't understand these countries, how likely are the people who live there to accept our advice on how they should be governed?

Why are we so sure that we know how each developing country should develop? Americans would never put their most important decisions in the hands of a foreign government. We don't even trust our own government.* Is it really our responsibility to bring justice to the people of Tibet, Taiwan, Kuwait, Kosovo, and Kashmir? How much money should we spend and how many lives put at risk on behalf of these places? The true source of America's exceptionalism is the drive to create a more perfect union at home, a subject of considerable neglect in recent years, and the moral compromises and ugly contradictions of our foreign policy undermine international perceptions of who we really are and what we believe.

Perhaps Americans are finally beginning to catch on. Remember that poll published in December 2013 by the Pew Research Center and the Council on Foreign Relations? The one that detailed what the report's authors called "the most lopsided balance in

---

* According to a poll conducted by CNN/ORC in July 2014, just 13 percent of Americans said they trust the federal government to do what is right "just about always" or most of the time. http://i2.cdn.turner.com/cnn/2014/images/08/08/rel7g.pdf.

favor of the U.S. 'minding its own business' in the nearly 50-year history of the measure"?[21] A CNN/ORC International poll released that same month found that 82 percent of Americans opposed the war in Afghanistan, making it the most unpopular conflict in U.S. history.

We can't promote democracy abroad while ignoring the popular will at home.

Damage at Home

Freedom is fragile. Americans must protect it right here at home. For all the damage a foolish foreign policy inflicts on U.S. interests abroad, the greatest damage is done inside the United States. First, a strong interventionist foreign policy strengthens the federal government in ways that distort the constitutionally prescribed balance of power between Washington and the states. The country's founders believed that dividing rights and responsibilities between the federal and state governments protects personal freedom and allows the states to serve as political and economic laboratories for the benefit of all Americans. Our superhero foreign policy draws rivers of taxpayer dollars toward the center, empowering Washington at the expense of local governments.

It also empowers the president at the expense of Congress in ways that upset the balance that the authors of the Constitution took great pains to design. Our superhero foreign policy has weakened not only our economy and our international reputation but also the respect of our leaders for America's founding principles. The founders did not intend to leave questions of war and peace in the hands of a single individual, even one who has won a national election. There are too many lives, too much money, and too many interests at stake to concentrate so much power in the executive. James Madison, who would later serve as president, wrote in 1793 that "the power to declare war, including the power of judging the causes of war, is fully and exclusively vested in the legislature. . . . The executive has no right, in any case, to decide the question, whether there is or is not cause for declaring war."[22] As Madison wrote to Thomas Jefferson in a letter in 1798:

> *The Constitution supposes what the history of all Governments demonstrates, that the executive is the branch of power most interested in war and most prone to it. It has accordingly with studied care vested the question of war in the Legislature.*[23]

Jefferson did not waver from this opinion even after becoming president, noting in 1805 that "Congress alone is constitutionally invested with the power of changing our condition from peace to war."[24] This argument appears again each time a president begins talking about using the country's military might. Too often, Americans form their opinions on war powers and the proper roles of the president and Congress based mainly on the strength of their own allegiance to the president's political party. America can't afford that sort of complacency. Not with so many lives and taxpayer dollars at stake. On questions of war and peace, Congress is not an inconvenience. It is the guarantor of our security and our liberties.

Our superhero foreign policy also poisons American democracy by intensifying the need for official secrecy. This problem comes in two forms. In an age when secrets are often exposed by whistle-blowers of various stripes and sophisticated cyber-activists, it has become increasingly difficult to hide the fact that America spies even on its allies. What happens to U.S. influence and prestige when our dirty secrets are exposed? Each foreign government will wonder whether our president was aware of this spying, and the answer is damning either way.

Our spy agencies also want to keep secret what they do within U.S. borders. Involvement in so many actual and potential conflicts overseas breeds fear that there are enemies within. In the 1950s, we feared infiltration by communists. Today it is terrorists. Why does America have seventeen different intelligence agencies?* Why are most of their budgets classified? How many U.S. companies work with them? How many taxpayer dollars are they sharing with foreign governments? Who exactly are the watchers watching? Who is watching the watchers? How can Americans hold their intelligence agencies accountable? There can be no "alert and knowledgeable citizenry" until the average American can answer at least some of these questions.

We are not allowed to know exactly how many Americans work for the U.S. Defense Department, how many bases our military operates overseas, or how many foreign countries host them. As a result, we don't really know how much of our money our Defense Department spends each year, but we can say with confidence that our superhero foreign policy diverts resources away from those parts of our economy that promote and protect prosperity. According to a Harvard University study published in 2013, the wars in Iraq and Afghanistan will cost Americans between $4 trillion and $6 trillion when "long-term medical care and disability

---

* The seventeen U.S. intelligence agencies include the Central Intelligence Agency, the National Security Agency, the Defense Intelligence Agency, the State Department's Bureau of Intelligence and Research, Air Force Intelligence, the FBI's National Security Branch, Army Intelligence and Security Command, the Department of Energy Office of Intelligence and Counterintelligence, Coast Guard Intelligence, the Treasury's Office of Intelligence and Analysis, the Drug Enforcement Administration, Marine Corps Intelligence, the National Geospatial-Intelligence Agency, the National Reconnaissance Office, the Office of Naval Intelligence, the Department of Homeland Security Office of Intelligence and Analysis, and the Office of the Director of National Intelligence.

compensation for service members, veterans and families, military replenishment and social and economic costs" are added to the more direct costs of combat operations.[25] Without cutting other defense spending, how many schools, homes, and hospitals might $4 trillion have built? How might our economy have responded over the past decade if we had simply left that $4 trillion in the taxpayer's pocket? Why are we investing in other countries when so many of those dollars are needed in our own country? Americans were asking this question before Dwight Eisenhower became president. Decades later, there is still no good answer.

What About Trade?

Doesn't our superhero foreign policy enhance American prosperity by creating opportunities for trade that boost our economy? It should be clear by now that expanded cross-border commerce isn't an absolute good for American workers. Trade agreements have the *potential* to benefit all who participate in them, but too often deals negotiated by political elites on behalf of economic elites overwhelmingly benefit elites—and they widen the gap between rich and poor in ways that further polarize American society. Enhanced trade with Mexico and China has killed large numbers of manufacturing jobs. That's good for the companies that can lower their production costs by outsourcing jobs. It's not so good for the millions of Americans thrown out of work as a result.

Before we commit our country to a new generation of trade deals, let's revisit the North American Free Trade Agreement. To mark the twentieth anniversary of NAFTA in early 2014, Public Citizen, a nonprofit think tank and advocacy group, published a report on the trade deal's economic impact.[26] The results were grim.

Before NAFTA was enacted, President Bill Clinton pledged that the agreement would create one million new U.S. jobs in the first five years of its life. Instead, according to Public Citizen, "U.S. firms used NAFTA's new foreign investor privileges to relocate production to Mexico to take advantage of that country's lower wages and weaker environmental standards . . . creating a massive new trade deficit that equated to an estimated net *loss* of one million U.S. jobs by 2004."[27]

Washington understood, of course, that changes brought about by NAFTA would "displace" significant numbers of workers. That's why the government created Trade Adjustment Assistance (TAA), a big federal program designed to train workers for new jobs and other industries. According to the Public Citizen report, more than 845,000 manufacturing workers have been certified for TAA since NAFTA took effect. But, warned the study, the TAA program isn't easy to qualify for and only covers some of the jobs lost.

In addition, NAFTA drove wages lower as workers were forced to accept whatever new jobs they could find. This problem was not limited to sectors directly impacted by NAFTA. As fired workers went looking for work in other industries, like food service and hospitality, jobs that can't be "offshored" to Mexico or China, they pushed down wages in those sectors too, according to the study. Nor did NAFTA lower food prices, easing the pain for consumers with less income. In fact, according to Public Citizen, "Despite a 188 percent rise in food imports from Canada and Mexico under NAFTA, the average nominal price of food in the United States jumped 65 percent since NAFTA went into effect." All these factors are helping to increase the gap between rich and poor in America and to shrink our middle class. We shouldn't be surprised then that many Americans surveyed by polling firm Angus Reid Public

Opinion in 2012 were sour on the benefits of NAFTA for workers and the broader U.S. economy. According to the results, significant percentages felt the deal had been "good for manufacturers (47%), employers (45%) and tourists (40%)." Just 34 percent said that NAFTA had benefited the U.S. economy, and 25 percent said it had been "good for workers."[28]

At least NAFTA benefited Mexico, you might think. Not so, said a 2009 study by the Carnegie Endowment for International Peace.[29] According to the study's authors, "The evidence points overwhelmingly to the conclusion that Mexico's reforms, backed by NAFTA, have largely been a disappointment for the country. Despite dramatic increases in trade and foreign investment, economic growth has been slow and job creation has been weak." The more recent Public Citizen report adds, "Despite promises that NAFTA would benefit Mexican consumers by granting access to cheaper imported products, the cost of basic consumer goods in Mexico has risen to seven times the pre-NAFTA level, while the minimum wage stands at only four times the pre-NAFTA level." It's unclear why prices rose, but it's clear that they did, despite the promises of NAFTA's champions. That's been bad news for impoverished Mexicans—and bad news for low-wage American workers who find themselves competing for work against illegal immigrants crossing the U.S.-Mexican border in search of a better life for themselves and their families.

Finally, trade is just one more aspect of U.S. foreign policy that focuses too much power in the hands of a single individual. As part of his plan to negotiate a Trans-Pacific Partnership, a colossal U.S.-led trade deal involving a dozen countries on either side of the Pacific, President Obama has called on Congress to give him "Trade Promotion Authority," popularly known as "fast track." This would grant him the power to negotiate a deal with all these other governments and to put the final draft before Congress for a simple up-or-down vote. No member of Congress is allowed to ask for any changes to the agreement or offer amendments to its text. Presidents of both parties have used this power in the past to get the deals that they and their supporters want without interference from individual lawmakers.

Why should we trust any president, Republican or Democrat, with authority to make decisions affecting the lives and livelihoods of so many millions of Americans without vital input from Congress? Shouldn't the American people and their representatives have a more direct say in the content of the big trade deals that define the parameters of our prosperity? Trade creates winners and losers within every country that participates, even if it's good for a country's economy as a whole. Every American deserves to know the details hidden in these deals.

The Ultimate Fear

Democracy is a living thing, and it can't be built like a wall. It's a continual process, a political ecosystem, a permanent revolution—one that can move backward as well as forward. It requires Eisenhower's "alert and knowledgeable citizenry" and a long-term, open-ended commitment to check the power of government. Our democracy depends on respect for our liberties and a healthy balance between Washington's authority and the rights of the fifty states. Government has no right to listen to your phone calls, read your e-mail, collect your bank records, or follow you through the Internet without good cause. These are violations of the constitutional right of American citizens to be "secure in their persons, houses, papers, and effects, against unreasonable searches and seizures." Nor should your government be allowed to detain you indefinitely without trial.

Yet all these values remain under threat, because various pieces of post-9/11 legislation have attempted to expand the government's ability to do all these things. The greatest threat that a superhero foreign policy poses for American democracy comes not from the enormous debt it imposes or even the heightened threat of terrorism itself, but from the potential impact of another large-scale attack on U.S. soil on the rights and privacy of American citizens. It is not China or Russia or Iran or any other emerging power or rogue state that threatens our freedom. The only government on earth that can strip Americans of their civil liberties is headquartered in Washington, D.C.

In short, there is no greater threat to American freedom and our civil liberties than a fear-driven response to a new terrorist attack and the misguided foreign policy response it might provoke. The attacks of September 11, 2001, created a new kind of fear for the average American, one that seemed to demand a forceful response of historic scale. The toppling of the Taliban in Afghanistan wasn't a satisfying enough answer. Our government went in search of other villains. The result: the two longest and most expensive wars in U.S. history.

Beyond the costs imposed on our military is the price we have paid at home. As more revelations emerge about the thousand ways in which our government now monitors our lives, we face a disturbing truth—Americans are not even legally entitled to know how much of our privacy we have surrendered. Security cameras we once would have rejected as Orwellian are now a fact of daily American life. U.S. companies with familiar names share data about our private lives and personal choices with the government we have empowered to protect us. How much more of our freedom will we hand over to faceless bureaucrats the next time a gang of jihadis hits the jackpot? What do all those cameras and the salaries of officials charged with monitoring them cost the American taxpayer? And how much more of our privacy will we surrender in years to come?

It is not power that makes America exceptional. It is freedom. Our freedom is at risk, and we must protect it.

Independent America—Democracy in One Country

Those who want Washington to police the planet and remake the world in America's image dismiss those who disagree with them as "isolationists." This word, this expletive, is not meant to shed light but to close conversation. It's a dismissal of every legitimate reservation that ordinary Americans have about the obvious foreign policy excesses and costly miscalculations of their government. Worst of all, it's an accusation that those who believe these excesses and mistakes damage our country are simply "rejectionists," carping critics with no positive vision.

That charge is false. Those who want Washington to declare our independence from the responsibility to solve everyone else's problems believe that America has profound untapped potential. Imagine what might become possible if we redirected the attention, energy, and resources that we now squander on a failed superhero foreign policy toward building the America we imagine, one that empowers all its people to realize their human potential. We stand on the verge of a crucial historic choice. We can continue to spend too much of our wealth and resources and too many American lives in a vain attempt to micromanage the evolution of global politics. Or we can rededicate ourselves to realizing the vision of our founders, one built atop respect for individual liberty and the awesome potential it creates for positive change.

Americans—genuine conservatives, true-blue liberals, and everyone in between—believe in freedom. We believe that there is no legitimate government without the consent of the governed. We also believe that these rights should be universal. But we know—or ought to know—that other societies have other values, and that we can't simply force our faith on others no matter how certain we are that our system is best. The best way to promote our ideas and values around the world is not by bribing or blackmailing other governments to accept them, or by imposing them at gunpoint, but by rededicating ourselves to perfecting democracy at home. It is within our power to build "democracy in one country." Our country. Only by building an America that lives up to its best ideals can we expect the citizens of other nations to demand that their governments follow America's lead.

By abandoning the ambitions of our leaders to police the world, we can invest much more to protect the homeland from the game-changing terrorist attack that might push America permanently off course. We can devote much more money toward rebuilding our infrastructure, creating the education system that the next generation of Americans deserves, and caring properly for those who have worn our country's uniform, while leaving enough in the taxpayer's pocket to power our economy into the future.

First, we must rationalize military spending. That means defending against tomorrow's true threats. To build and maintain the military we need for the twenty-first century, it is far more important to spend wisely than to spend more. We must devote our resources not to the expensive weapons that helped us win the wars of the past but to the lighter, smarter weapons needed to combat terrorist and other threats to the homeland that we are sure to face in years to come. Tomorrow's wars will be waged not with aircraft carriers and heavy bombers but with information—and the intelligence and expertise needed to understand and use it. They will be won less often on land or sea than in financial markets and in cyberspace.

We must never forget that national security begins at home. To secure the homeland, we must finally make the investments needed to protect our borders, ports, airports, and public infrastructure against terrorist attack. But we must also invest in our country's resilience, our ability to bounce back from disasters, natural or unnatural, and continue building a safer and more prosperous America. We must increase public awareness of the threats we face and how to manage them—at the federal and local levels and in every American home and workplace.

Finally, a word on immigration. Illegal immigration is a serious problem in need of a serious solution. But we must always continue to welcome those who would come to this country legally, as millions have done since our founding. The best and brightest, those hungry for a better life and willing to work for it, have always made the United States stronger. That is true not just for high-skilled workers from developed nations, but for those from poorer countries who have never had a chance to show what they can do. Immigrants add not only to the skills of our workforce but to the nation's innovative potential. Make them Americans. Educate their children. Celebrate their successes and all that it means for our future. Closing our borders to terrorists must never mean closing our country's doors to those who enter the United States legally seeking a better life.

Rebuild Our Public Infrastructure

Why are we investing in public infrastructure in Afghanistan or Iraq instead of at home?

We must rebuild our shamefully crumbling physical infrastructure. In their book *That Used to Be Us: How America Fell Behind in the World It Invented and How We Can Come Back*, authors Thomas L. Friedman and Michael Mandelbaum reported on an alarming 2009 study from the American Society of Civil Engineers (ASCE) called "A Report Card for America's Infrastructure." The study gave the United States an overall grade of D, noting that little had changed in the quality of America's roads, bridges, rail, dams, drinking water, and other elements of public infrastructure since the organization's previous study in 2005, other than the amount of money needed to improve them. In 2005, the ASCE estimated that it would cost $1.6 trillion to repair the country's infrastructure. By 2009, that figure had risen to $2.2 trillion.[30]

Fast-forward four years. In 2013, the ASCE issued another update, one that provides estimates of the funding needed by 2020 to "maintain a state of good repair," the equivalent of a grade of B, in these same categories of public infrastructure. The latest report elevated America's overall score from D to D+ but increased the estimated cost of investment needed to achieve that goal to $3.6 trillion. Categories included aviation, bridges, dams, drinking water, energy, hazardous waste, inland waterways, levees, ports, public parks and recreation, rail, roads, schools, solid waste management, transit, and wastewater. Solid waste scored a B–, while grades in the other fifteen categories ranged from C+ to D–.

The economic impact of this failure can be measured. According to the report, "The Federal Aviation Administration (FAA) estimates that the national cost of airport congestion and delays was almost $22 billion in 2012. If current federal funding levels are maintained, the FAA anticipates that the cost of congestion and delays to the economy will rise from $34 billion in 2020 to $63 billion by 2040." In addition, "deficient and deteriorating transit systems cost the U.S. economy $90 billion in 2010," and "forty-two percent of America's major urban highways remain congested, costing the economy an estimated $101 billion in wasted time and fuel annually."[31] This is one small corner of a much larger and more frightening problem.

Invest in American Education

The ASCE had similar dire warnings about the state of America's schools:

> Public school enrollment is projected to gradually increase through 2019, yet state and local school construction funding continues to decline. National spending on school construction has diminished to approximately $10 billion in 2012, about half the level spent prior to the recession, while the condition of school facilities continues to be a significant concern for communities. Experts now estimate the investment needed to modernize and maintain our nation's school facilities is at least $270 billion or more. However, due to the absence of national data on school facilities for more than a decade, a complete picture of the condition of our nation's schools remains mostly unknown.[32]

Our failure to invest properly in the education of our children extends well beyond the money we spend on buildings and equipment. Every three years, American fifteen-year-olds participate in the Programme for International Student Assessment (PISA), a test given by the Organisation for Economic Co-operation and Development to more than half a million students in sixty-five countries. Students are tested in reading, math, and science. The most recent test, given in 2012, produced predictably mediocre results for Americans, who scored at or below average in all three areas. More worrying, the results suggest that students in many other countries are improving their scores while there is little change in U.S. results, a formula for future failure.[33]

By bringing the money we spend abroad back home, we will have the resources we need to build safe, state-of-the-art schools with state-of-the-art teaching tools. We can invest more money in better wages for our teachers to ensure that the profession attracts smart, talented, and creative men and women who might otherwise enter other professions in search of better-paying jobs. There is ample evidence that better-paid teachers produce better results in the classroom.[34] We can reduce class sizes across the country to ensure that educators spend less time policing behavior and more time teaching. Aware that a hungry student is more likely to have trouble concentrating, we can provide students with nutritious meals. We should also invest not just in schools but in preschools to give our kids a critical head start.

Care for Our Veterans

By bringing the money home, we will finally provide our veterans with the first-rate health care they deserve. As of this writing, hundreds of thousands of those who have served in this country's wars are trapped in a bureaucratic nightmare that frustrates their ability to receive the physical, mental, and emotional health care they need. Veterans of the war in Vietnam, who make up nearly 40 percent of those filing new benefit claims, now face a wide variety of health challenges related to advanced age. Another 20 percent of claims comes from service members returning from Iraq and Afghanistan. We will be investing enormous sums in their care for decades to come; payments to veterans of World War I did not peak until more than half a century after that war ended.[35]

It's not enough to think generously. We must also think creatively. Instead of pouring more money into a Veterans Administration that is not equipped to care for the growing numbers who need help, we should follow the wise counsel of retired colonel Jack Jacobs, one of America's most distinguished veterans. Colonel Jacobs has argued persuasively that those who have served our country deserve better than the VA can provide. "There is no reason that veterans who would otherwise wait for months to be seen at a VA health clinic can't be seen by private doctors, the same doctors who treat everyone else," he wrote in May 2014. "The procedure doesn't need to be complicated: patient is seen by private doctor, private doctor treats patient, doctor sends bill to government, government pays doctor." As Jacobs points out, "We already have Medicare and Medicaid, which could serve as templates for a veterans program without facilities or physicians."[36] Without a superhero foreign policy to finance and manage, government will have more money and more time to think through these challenges.

Put the Money Back in the Taxpayer's Pocket

Finally, we can leave more money in the taxpayer's pocket. Never has it been more important to allow Americans to keep more of what they earn. America's recovery from the Great Recession has been painfully slow, in part because millions of Americans are still so busy digging out of personal debt and putting aside the extra dollar to rebuild their retirement savings that consumer spending remains much less than it should be. Instead of sending their money to Washington so that policymakers can use it to play international superhero, let ordinary Americans use it to stimulate growth, create jobs, and reexpand the country's beleaguered middle class. There is no better stimulus plan.

For all these reasons, it is time for Americans to declare their independence from a foreign policy that bankrupts our treasury, depletes our energy, undermines both our credibility and our self-confidence, and cannot be sustained. As Ike warned in his farewell address to the nation, "We . . . must avoid the impulse to live only for today, plundering for our own ease and convenience the precious resources of tomorrow. We cannot mortgage the material assets of our grandchildren without risking the loss also of their political and spiritual heritage. We want democracy to survive for all generations to come, not to become the insolvent phantom of tomorrow."

Let us declare independence from commitments abroad that undermine our democracy and compromise our values. Let us better understand the world before we try to remake it, define our national interest modestly, and make American peace and prosperity a model for other nations.

Let's return to the quiz you took in the introduction. Here is how a champion of Independent America might answer (in italics with a brief explanation for that choice).

An Independent America Answer Key

1. Freedom is:

    a. The right of every human being.

    b. Fragile. Americans must protect it right here at home.

    c. In the eye of the beholder.

We cannot effectively preach democracy abroad until we practice it at home.

2. America is:

    a. Exceptional because of what it represents.

    b. Exceptional because of all it has done for the world.

    c. Not an exceptional nation. America is the most powerful, but that doesn't mean it's always right.

Our example is more powerful than our most powerful weapons.

3. Which of these statements best expresses your opinion?

    a. America will be better off if we mind our own business and let other countries get along the best they can.

    b. America must lead.

c. The primary purpose of U.S. foreign policy should be to make America safer and more prosperous.

We can't build and sustain a risky and expensive foreign policy without lasting public support, and that support is no longer there.

4. China is:

a. America's greatest challenge and greatest opportunity.

b. **The place where too many American jobs have gone.**

c. The world's largest dictatorship.

We have much less influence with China's leaders and the Chinese people than we like to think. Let's devote our time, energy, and resources to restoring the strength of our economy.

5. America's biggest problem in the Middle East is that:

a. Washington supports the region's dictators rather than its people.

b. Washington ignores small problems until they turn into big ones.

c. **Washington believes it can manage an unmanageable region.**

It's time to accept that we can never bring peace and stability to the Middle East.

6. U.S. spy capabilities:

a. Will always be a double-edged sword.

b. *Threaten our privacy.*

c. Are vital for protecting America.

Compromising the principles on which our nation was founded will not make us safer.

7. The primary responsibility of the president of the United States is:

a. To advance U.S. interests at home and abroad.

b. *To promote, protect, and defend the Constitution of the United States.*

c. To lead.

We are a nation governed by laws, not by men and women. May it ever be so.

8. Which of the following best expresses your view?

a. A great leader can change the world.

b. *A great leader must lead by example.*

c. In the real world, any leader must often choose the least bad of many bad options.

We cannot ask others to follow our example until we live up to our own ideals.

9. Which is the most at risk?

a. America's economy.

b. America's international reputation.

c. *The respect of our leaders for America's founding principles.*

Our Constitution and our faith in rule of law have created our economic strength and international influence.

10. I hope that by the year 2050:

a. America will share the burdens of leadership with reliable, like-minded allies.

b. *Americans will have created a more perfect union at home.*

c. American leadership will have helped as many people as possible around the world topple the tyrants who deny them the freedom they deserve.

Americans are builders. We must never stop building the America we deserve.

CHAPTER 4

Moneyball America
To Promote and Protect American Value

Reason is a very light rider, and easily shook off.
—Jonathan Swift

Y ou're standing on the bow of an enormous ship, an international oil tanker set to pass through the world's most dangerous choke point. It's a clear day, and you can see both shores—Oman to the south and Iran to the north. A crew member tells you that at its narrowest point, the strait is just twenty-one miles wide, but because the vessel is so big, you'll be following the other thirteen ships running this gauntlet today inside a shipping lane in the center of the channel that's just *two* miles wide for much of the journey.[1]

Your new friend points left toward Iran and tells you that there are soldiers onshore watching as you pass. They're close enough that if they decide to attack, they won't need high-tech weapons. They won't even need radar. He tells you that, given the narrow sea lanes, it would be easy for Iran to stop traffic with a few well-placed mines in the water. Facing forward, you see both U.S. and Iranian naval vessels ahead. You might even see the Iranians playing chicken with U.S. ships—and the Americans firing water cannons to keep them at a safe distance. You *won't* see the U.S. submarine protecting today's traffic from below. Sensing that he's spooked you, your crewmate tells you that the United States and Iran haven't fired at one another in anger in these waters since 1988. Sensing your relief, he quickly adds that the strait offers an ideal target for terrorists.

Why the big U.S. naval presence? About 20 percent of the world's traded oil travels through the Strait of Hormuz every day. Closing this narrow passage would send global oil prices surging toward panic levels within a matter of hours. For someone looking to attack every energy-importing country in the world, this is a great place to do it. Iran has warned several times over the years that it might block tanker traffic in retaliation for U.S. and European actions it doesn't like, and its top naval commander warned in December 2011 that closing the strait would be "easier than drinking a glass of water."* It's the job of the U.S. Fifth Fleet, based 350 miles away in Bahrain, to ensure that that doesn't happen.

Why must the United States accept responsibility for keeping these threats at bay? After all, America needs this oil much less than China does. More than three-quarters of the oil passing through the strait today is headed for Asia. Just 12 percent is headed for the Americas, and 8 percent for Europe.[2] U.S. dependence on this oil will fall further as new energy technologies and higher U.S. fuel

---

* There have been attacks in the past. During the Iran-Iraq War in the 1980s, both sides mined the strait. An Iranian mine nearly sank an American frigate in 1988. During the first Gulf War in 1990-91, Iraq placed more than thirteen hundred mines in the northern Persian Gulf, badly damaging two U.S. warships.

efficiency standards take effect. In fact, crude oil is now produced in thirty-one U.S. states, a record number.[3] As noted earlier, breakthroughs in unconventional energy production will help ensure that America continues down the path of energy independence; depending on the price of oil, it could even achieve that feat by 2019. It became the world's largest oil producer back in 2014, and has been the world's largest natural gas producer since 2010.[4]

Arguably, Iran needs the strait open more than the United States does. Its own energy exports are crucial for its government revenue, and given how much of that oil and gas is headed for China, Beijing would apply intense political and economic pressure on Iran not to attack the strait or its traffic. Even the threat of such an action would push insurance rates higher, raising costs for China in particular.

Yet no one can afford to take free passage through the strait for granted. If Iran, or anyone else, closed it for a month, the economic shock would be felt around the world, including in the United States. Though we need less of that oil than we used to, we'll depend on the strait for significant volumes for years to come. And today's interconnected global economy ensures that even if America were isolated from the first economic shock wave, we would surely feel the second—and sooner rather than later. Ensuring the strait remains open for business is a long-term commitment that only the United States can make. That isn't going to change in the next ten years. George Washington urged future presidents and lawmakers to resist foreign entanglements, but America's first president never dreamed of this problem.

* * * * * * *

U.S. foreign policy should be designed to make the United States safer and more prosperous; it's foolish to think that Americans can safeguard their interests and promote prosperity without accepting *some* costs and risks far beyond our borders. The ideas expressed in the previous chapter won't create an "Independent America." This is Isolationist America, a shining city on a hill built high atop Fantasy Island. There are things that must be done, and it's in America's national interest for Americans to do.

To safeguard U.S. national security, Washington must lead coalitions of the willing, able, and like-minded to block the proliferation of nuclear weapons and to use any means necessary to deny terrorists the tools they need for a catastrophic attack on U.S. soil. Because the fate of the U.S. economy is tied to that of the world economy, U.S. foreign policy must promote and protect global growth, both by minimizing the risk of war and by giving as many countries as possible a stake in stability through commerce and investment. To safeguard prosperity at home, Washington must forge new trade and investment ties. And we must accomplish all this while living within our means.

It's true that America's elected leaders cannot conduct an ambitious foreign policy without U.S. public support. Yet if that support doesn't exist today, it's because our elected leaders have done a poor job of explaining why certain things must be done, why the United States must do them, and how those things protect and serve our most vital interests. Afghanistan and Iraq have soured the American people on potentially costly commitments abroad. But these two poorly designed foreign policy adventures do not represent the best we can do. We cannot shrink from the future. There will be more threats, more costs, and more opportunities, and U.S. policymakers must be prepared to confront them.

In 2003, author Michael Lewis wrote a bestselling book called *Moneyball: The Art of Winning an Unfair Game.*[5] It's the story of how Billy Beane, general manager of the cash-strapped Oakland A's baseball club, used a hyperrational, rigorous approach to build a winning franchise. The need to do more with less persuaded Beane to question every old assumption, kill every sacred cow, look beyond the familiar, and reinvent the way that successful teams are built.

A Moneyball foreign policy relies on a cold-blooded, interest-driven approach that redefines America's role in the world in a way designed to maximize the return on the taxpayer's investment. It recognizes that we have a few responsibilities that no one else can accept, but everywhere possible it sheds burdens in favor of opportunities and focuses our leaders on protecting the bottom line. We can't police every corner, and Moneyball promotes America's *value,* not its values. It comes much closer than isolationist dogma to answering President Eisenhower's call for a rational foreign policy approach that makes America both more secure and more prosperous.

Security

The toughest choice any president makes is whether to go to war, and our past reluctance to fight has served us well. Those who support the Independent America argument are right that it wasn't simply victory in the two world wars but our late entry into them that made the United States a superpower. By waiting as long as we could before joining these fights in faraway lands, we enhanced America's political influence and economic power relative to every potential rival. Yet we mustn't forget the years between the wars when isolationist U.S. policymakers thought Americans could simply retreat to a world that didn't need American leadership. Washington should never wage war where it's not vital to U.S. interests, but nor should we shrink from any fight when it's clear that our safety and prosperity are at stake. Let's also remember that the credible *threat* of force is an essential element of successful diplomacy. If Washington is to conduct the effective (and cost-effective) Moneyball foreign policy that Americans will demand in the twenty-first century, our elected leaders will need a state-of-the-art military. They'll also need a clear and consistent set of guidelines to help them decide when war is the last best means of defending U.S. interests.

Fortunately, Colin Powell has provided one. As chairman of the Joint Chiefs of Staff and secretary of state, Powell served as both America's top soldier and its top diplomat. The so-called Powell doctrine, first articulated in 1990, is an elaboration on a similar framework created by former defense secretary Caspar Weinberger. Powell's version, based largely on lessons learned from the war in Vietnam, provides a set of commonsense decision-making principles that reflect shrewd Moneyball thinking.

When a president and Congress are considering war, they must answer the following questions:

1. Is a vital national security interest threatened?

2. Do we have a clear and attainable objective?

3. Have the risks and costs been fully and frankly analyzed?

4. Have all other nonviolent policy means been fully exhausted?

5. Is there a plausible exit strategy to avoid endless entanglement?

6. Have the consequences of U.S. action been fully considered?

7. Is the action supported by the American people?

8. Do we have genuine broad international support?

If the answer to any of these questions is no, war is not the answer.

With these questions in mind, compare America's two wars with Iraq's Saddam Hussein. In August 1990, Iraqi forces invaded neighboring Kuwait and crossed the border into Saudi Arabia, briefly occupying the Saudi city of Khafji in the country's oil-rich Eastern Province before Saudi and Qatari forces, backed by U.S. marines, drove them out. President George H. W. Bush ordered Saddam to withdraw his forces from Kuwait. Saddam refused, and in January 1991, U.S. forces ousted the Iraqi military from that country and imposed sanctions designed to cripple Iraq's economy.

Twelve years later, a second President Bush launched a second war, one designed to topple Saddam, find and destroy Iraq's weapons of mass destruction, and plant the seeds of democracy. These two wars illustrate the difference between a Moneyball foreign policy that was intelligently designed to serve the U.S. national interest and one that falls short of this high standard in every respect. Take these questions one by one.

Was a vital national security interest threatened? In 1990, by seizing control of oil production in Kuwait, and perhaps in eastern Saudi Arabia, Saddam would have controlled a large enough share of the world's oil to send the U.S. economy into recession simply by cutting output to drive energy prices higher. In that sense, Saddam threatened a vital U.S. interest—as well as the economies of oil-importing countries around the world. But after the war in 1991, Saddam would never again threaten a vital U.S. national security interest, because sanctions deprived him of the means to build weapons of mass destruction. As important, during the second war, U.S. troops remained in Iraq for eight years after Saddam had been defeated, as part of an effort to stabilize and rebuild Iraq, though the insurgency that grew from the ashes of the war did not threaten America's national security.

Did the United States have a clear and attainable objective? In 1991, the answer was yes. The elder President Bush's objective was to eject Saddam's forces from Kuwait and cripple his government by isolating its economy. The U.S.-led war drove the Iraqis home within days, and sanctions were imposed that Saddam was never able to fully escape. In 2003, the answer was no. There was no clear and attainable objective. Saddam was removed from power, and the war's purpose became unclear when no weapons of mass destruction were discovered. The occupation of Iraq did nothing to make America safer or more prosperous.

Were the risks and costs fully and frankly analyzed? In 1991, the central debate among policymakers was whether to pursue Iraqi troops all the way to Baghdad and capture Saddam. After weighing the question, President Bush determined that the risks and costs associated with a war inside Iraq and the need to rebuild the country under new leadership were too high. The younger President Bush did not fully analyze the question of Iraq's weapons of mass destruction, and he failed to realistically weigh the costs of a long-term occupation of Iraq on American lives, the U.S. treasury, or America's international reputation.

Were all other nonviolent policy means fully exhausted? In 1991, Saddam could have avoided war by cutting a face-saving deal that included voluntary withdrawal from Kuwait. Unappealing as that choice may have been, the alternative was a fight he couldn't win. Maybe he didn't understand that. Aware that Saddam would not back down, President Bush could either have allowed him to maintain his hold on Kuwait's oil supply—with all the new power that would have given him—or go to war. In 2003, the younger President Bush had an option that his father never really had: He could have done nothing. He might well have determined that Saddam remained trapped inside the box that Bush's father had built for him and that leaving him in isolation better served U.S. interests than did a poorly conceived war. In short, Iraq's invasion of Kuwait made the first war all but inevitable. The second was a war of choice.

Was there a plausible exit strategy to avoid endless entanglement? Here the contrast is most obvious. In 1991, the elder President Bush committed U.S. troops to a war that began on February 24. Iraqi troops were forced from Kuwait by February 28. A formal cease-fire ended the conflict on March 3, and troops began arriving home on March 17. The second war erupted in March 2003, and the last U.S. soldiers departed Iraq in December 2011. The father's war lasted less than a month. The son's lasted nearly nine years.

Were the consequences of U.S. action fully considered? No one who orders troops into battle can foresee every consequence of that decision, but here again the differences are stark. The elder President Bush intended to evict Iraqi forces from Kuwait, prevent an invasion of Saudi Arabia, restore stability in the region, bring the troops home, and impose sanctions, thanks in part to the wise counsel of National Security Adviser Brent Scowcroft. An interview with Scowcroft published in 2005 makes clear the difference between a foreign policy decision based on careful calculation of U.S. interests and one based on moral outrage or public support for action:

> Though the President had employed the rhetoric of moral necessity to make the case for war [in 1990], Scowcroft said, he would not let his feelings about good and evil dictate the advice he gave the President. It would have been no problem for America's military to reach Baghdad, he said. The problems would have arisen when the Army entered the

Iraqi capital. "At the minimum, we'd be an occupier in a hostile land," he said. "Our forces would be sniped at by guerrillas, and, once we were there, how would we get out? What would be the rationale for leaving? I don't like the term 'exit strategy'—but what do you do with Iraq once you own it?"[6]

U.S. military action in the Middle East will always generate hostility, and the presence of American soldiers in Saudi Arabia, the sacred land of Mecca and Medina, during the first war with Iraq is thought to have fueled the anger of Osama bin Laden and other Islamist militants.[7]

But it was the second war that produced direct and dramatic negative consequences for U.S. interests. Far from being "greeted as liberators," U.S. soldiers found themselves drawn into a conflict that lasted longer than World War II. In March 2003, Deputy Secretary of State Paul Wolfowitz told Congress that Iraq could "finance its own reconstruction" via oil exports.[8] The administration projected that the war would cost U.S. taxpayers between $50 billion and $60 billion, including the cost of rebuilding the country. In 2013, the Costs of War Project, a nonprofit organization affiliated with Brown University, estimated that the war had actually cost $1.7 trillion.[9] Add the long-term price tag for veterans' benefits, and the price rises to more than $2 trillion. There is no credible argument that the second Bush administration understood the most basic costs and consequences of that war—for U.S. taxpayers, U.S. soldiers, our coalition partners, or Iraqis.

Were the actions supported by the American people? In January 1991, President George H. W. Bush's plan to go to war won the backing of 55 percent of Americans in a Pew Research poll. Speedy victory drove that number to 80 percent, though a recession helped ensure that he lost his bid for reelection in 1992. A dozen years later, his son had even broader prewar support. Another Pew Research poll found that 77 percent of Americans supported the 2003 invasion of Iraq. But how did these wars wear over time? In 2001, ten years after the first war, 63 percent of Americans said the first President Bush had made the right decision in going to war. Just 31 percent disagreed.[10] In April 2008, Pew found that just 37 percent supported the still-active second war with Iraq with 57 percent opposed.[11] Both presidents had the public backing they needed to go to war. The younger Bush could not sustain support for a commitment he should have known would last for years.

Did these two wars have broad international support? The first war could claim the support of more than thirty foreign governments. Fourteen of them contributed at least one thousand military personnel. The second war had the initial support of an even larger number of governments, though only Britain, Australia, Spain, Italy, Ukraine, and Georgia contributed at least one thousand of their citizens to the effort. But the younger President Bush moved forward despite fierce opposition from NATO allies France and Germany. UN secretary-general Kofi Annan said in 2004 that from the point of view of the UN Charter, the second U.S.-led war on Saddam was "illegal."[12] Saddam's 1990 invasion of Kuwait and the threat he posed for Saudi Arabia united much of the world behind the effort to oust him. The war to finish him off in 2003 had nothing like that kind of backing—and serious resistance from traditional U.S. allies.

War-weary Americans are sick of debates over Iraq, but if we are to build a foreign policy that truly serves our national interest, one that enjoys consistent popular support because it doesn't waste American lives or taxpayer dollars, we must learn the lessons that these two wars have to teach us. As secretary of state, Colin Powell played a major supporting role in selling the need to go to war in 2003. That should not discourage us from using the principles he created to help us decide when war is necessary and when it is not. Every American should set aside the political biases that too often distort our reason and blind us to the vital lessons of our past— especially those we can learn from our worst mistakes.

Bad Reasons to Fight

One of the most important of those lessons is that no leader or law-maker should ever treat a decision about war solely as a test of personal or national toughness. Russia's assault on Ukraine in 2014 undermined the case for an intelligently designed Moneyball foreign policy by persuading some in Washington that brute force is still the trump card in relations among nations. Russia's Vladimir Putin has cultivated the image of steely-eyed strongman over many years, and his aggressive action against former Soviet subjects—Georgia in 2008 and Ukraine in 2014—left some Americans disappointed when U.S. troops didn't ride in like the cavalry to punish his overreach and remind him who's boss. Some who criticized Obama were motivated by the demands of election-year politics, but others were driven by a dangerously expansive conception of American power and the responsibility to use it in places where it makes no sense.

A bias toward always "projecting strength" is a foolish basis for a foreign policy. In October 1962, President John F. Kennedy faced down pressure from some of his own senior military advisers to respond to the presence of Soviet missiles in Cuba with a U.S. invasion of that island. Fortunately, we'll never know how close the world came to nuclear war or how many American lives might have been lost in an effort to appear "resolute" and "strong." Instead, Kennedy used a defensive naval blockade of Cuba to prevent Soviet resupply and a backdoor diplomatic deal on U.S. weapons in Turkey to bring the Cold War's most dangerous direct confrontation to a peaceful conclusion. Tough-minded diplomacy, backed with the credible threat of force, carried the day. The nuclear threat was averted. Loss of life was limited to two American pilots.* Americans didn't have to pay for an unnecessary war.

Still, whenever an American president decides not to use force, there are opportunistic critics at home and abroad who say that the White House has made America look weak. Many who level that charge have selfish motives. Foreign detractors are often trying to pressure a president to act on their behalf. Domestic critics want the president they're attacking to lose the next election. Yet a truly strong leader cares only about acting in the country's interest. A Moneyball approach demands that we fight when and where we choose—and on our own terms.

Kennedy is far from the only president to find the courage to avoid useless confrontation. Before he was elected president in 1980, Democrats attacked Ronald Reagan, just as they had attacked Republican presidential nominee Barry Goldwater in 1964, as a reactionary, trigger-happy firebrand more likely to turn the Cold War hot than to achieve peace and prosperity. Yet one of President Reagan's wisest and most courageous foreign policy decisions was one that would have branded most presidents as cowards.

In June 1982, Israel invaded Lebanon. By the end of that summer, a multinational peacekeeping force of 800 U.S. marines, 800 Italian soldiers, and 400 French soldiers arrived in Beirut to safeguard the evacuation of Palestinian fighters from the country and

---

* U-2 pilot Major Rudy Anderson was shot down on the final day of the crisis. Captain Glenn Hyde was killed after the crisis when his reconnaissance plane developed a mechanical problem.

act as a buffer between warring factions. Over the next year, Lebanon's security deteriorated dramatically, and on October 23, 1983, a small group of Islamic militants launched one of history's most successful terrorist attacks. Early that morning, a suicide bomber drove a truck carrying more than ten tons of TNT into a barracks housing the multinational force. The attack killed 241 U.S. servicemen, the deadliest single-day loss of U.S. marines since the battle of Iwo Jima in 1945. Minutes later, a second truck bomb at another site killed 58 French paratroopers.[13]

Not surprisingly, President Reagan responded first with defiance, and some within his administration argued that links between the group claiming responsibility for the attacks and the government in Iran justified a U.S. attack on Iran's Revolutionary Guard Corps, a politically powerful branch of Iran's military. Defense Secretary Caspar Weinberger had failed to persuade Reagan that the insertion of U.S. marines was a bad idea, but he won the internal argument over the question of retaliating against Iran. The evidence of Iranian involvement was circumstantial, he insisted, and an attack could serve no useful purpose. Reagan also insisted that the marines would not "cut and run." He argued they must remain in Lebanon "until the situation is under control. . . . We have vital interests in Lebanon. And our actions in Lebanon are in the cause of world peace."

But by themselves, U.S. marines could never bring the situation under control, the United States did *not* have vital interests in Lebanon, the U.S. presence was *not* in the cause of world peace, and Reagan soon found the courage to change his mind. In February 1984, he ordered the withdrawal of the marines from Lebanon, and all had been evacuated within three weeks. Asked later what lesson had been learned from this episode, Weinberger said the following:

You have to have a mission; you have to know what you want to do; you have to use force as a last resort after everything else has failed; that when you use it, you have to use it at overwhelming strength, and win your objective and get out.[14]

That's the Weinberger doctrine, which established the basis for the Powell doctrine. It was inspired primarily by the war in Vietnam, but the deadly humiliation in Beirut brought that lesson home yet again. Yet the value of a Moneyball foreign policy is not simply in avoiding poorly conceived commitments that cost lives. It's also in having the courage to admit mistakes, to make the right corrective call, and to stand by it when critics, foreign and domestic, question your toughness and America's strength. We shouldn't go to war because the American people (or our president) are angry. We shouldn't go to war to appear resolute. We should never go to war to defend a principle. Building a winning foreign policy is not simply a matter of will. It's a test of vision and temperament.

Watch the Cost

The Independent America advocates are also right that we can't afford our current foreign policy. We must rationalize the costs. Though the United States is not and should never become an imperial power, we still spend more on our military than all our potential challengers *combined,* and we're investing too much in too many of the wrong weapons. The U.S. Navy is equipped with twelve aircraft carrier groups that allow Washington to project power in every region of the world, create jobs, and enhance our prestige. But this hardware can only counter conventional military threats from other governments; it's built to fight the wars of the last century. It gives presidents the ability to commit U.S. forces into conflicts best avoided, and it can't help us rebuild a country after we've removed its government. It does little to protect us from terrorists with chemical, biological, or nuclear weapons and nothing to protect us from cyber-attack. If China or Russia one day attacks the United States, they're much more likely to hit us in cyberspace than to use cruise missiles or nuclear submarines.

The United States can afford to remain the one nation with influence in every region of the world, but only if we rely on our partners to share the costs and risks. We can't afford to be the dominant voice in every neighborhood. Instead, a Moneyball foreign policy guides us to rely on willing and able friends and allies to build partnerships, ties that are based on respect for the interests, values, and preoccupations of all the major players in each region— including those who choose to remain outside these partnerships, even our enemies. When we discover on a particular issue that we have no willing allies, it's best to back off.

The best way to manage our costs is to stop trying to police every neighborhood. Instead, Washington should build and support regional balances of power.[15] The United States has interests in Latin America and in sub-Saharan Africa, but these regions pose little threat to U.S. national security or prosperity. Western Europe has no serious security challenges. That's why a Moneyball approach will guide America's next president to shrug off criticism that his security policy ignores these places, allowing him to focus almost entirely on East Asia, Eurasia, North Africa, and the Middle East.

In East Asia, the United States should pursue a strategic balance—in our approach to the region generally and to China in particular. First, Washington must strengthen both security and economic ties with China's neighbors—particularly Japan, South Korea, Indonesia, Vietnam, and the Philippines—not to prevent those countries from building solid commercial relations with China, but to allow them to do so without becoming economically dependent on Beijing. Those partners should understand, however, that the United States will not back them when they provoke China needlessly. U.S. support can never be unconditional. Washington must also strengthen trade and investment ties with China—to ensure that Americans continue to benefit from China's rise, to deepen the economic interdependence that promotes stability in the relationship and across the region, and to reassure Beijing that deeper U.S. involvement in East Asia need not come at China's expense. Those who support an Independent America will say that East Asia's rivalries are none of our business, while the Obama administration too often appears less than fully committed to any strategy at all. A Moneyball approach will lead us to rely more on trade and investment and less on security guarantees that we can't afford to honor indefinitely. America's economic and security interests demand a stable balance of power in East Asia, and only America can lead the effort to sustain one.

It's vital that once the president sets priorities, the administration must stick to them. Everyone knows that distractions are part of the job. But the Obama administration committed itself during the president's first term to that pivot to Asia, a plan to rebalance American security and trade policy toward a deeper focus on East Asia, in particular. Given that this region is more important than any other for the strength and resilience of the global economy over the next generation and that it has more than its share of dangerous rivalries, this was a wise plan, one completely consistent with a Moneyball approach to foreign policy.

In his second term, however, President Obama has allowed

himself to become distracted by a conflict in Syria that has monsters well represented on both sides, as well as a quixotic bid to establish an Israeli-Palestinian peace that neither side is ready to negotiate. The United States can't solve every problem. We must focus our attentions where they are best able to promote U.S. national security and economic opportunity. The next president must build an intelligently designed plan based on limited objectives—and stick to it. The pivot to Asia remains an excellent place to start.

When managing relations with Russia, a Moneyball approach requires that Washington let Europe take the lead. Given Russia's much deeper economic ties with Germany, Britain, and France, it is those countries whose interests are most directly at stake, and those that are best able to exact a political price for Russian aggression. National pride remains among the world's most powerful political forces. Attempts to play the world's policeman are far more likely than a Moneyball approach to arouse the sort of nationalist backlash that the Soviets faced in Eastern Europe—even within the Soviet Union itself—and that the United States encountered in Vietnam and Iraq. Let the Russians play the aggressor, undermining national pride among their neighbors. As defender of that pride, America can restore some of the credibility it has lost in other conflicts.[16]

That's not to say that the United States has no role to play in the Ukraine conflict. Washington can and should use sanctions and other affordable means of punishment to raise the cost for the Kremlin of every Russian action that Washington wants to discourage. But we can't afford the illusion that Washington has the power to isolate Russia or to change the Kremlin's behavior on any issue on which Moscow believes its core interests are at stake. The Independent America advocates will say that Russian actions do not threaten us and are not our concern, while those in our current government talk as if we have a moral responsibility to save Ukraine. Both are wrong. A Moneyball approach requires that we maximize return on minimal investment. We must directly confront Russia only if it attacks one of our formal alliance partners. Only America can give this threat the credibility it needs to deter hostile Russian action.

In the Middle East, the relationship that best defines the region's balance of power is the rivalry between Iran and Saudi Arabia. A Moneyball foreign policy will lead the United States to try to maintain open and constructive relations with both. Washington would do well to build a more pragmatic (if not always positive) relationship with Iran. This increases the importance of solidifying ties with Saudi Arabia. The Saudis want a clearer U.S. commitment to their security. The next U.S. president can provide one.

Building mutually profitable commercial and investment relationships with both of these countries will give Iranians the chance for prosperity they want, make it more difficult for their government to isolate them from the rest of the world, and give the Saudis the confidence they need to avoid a conflict with Iran that could ignite the entire Middle East. Finally, America should help bolster the security of Israel, the only reliable U.S. ally in the region, but Washington need not back every Israeli action against Palestinians. The Israelis have every right to kill those who threaten their citizens, but Israel's willingness to inflict mass casualties on Palestinian civilians does not serve U.S. interests. Americans need a stable balance of power in the Middle East, and only America can support one.

Fight Terrorism

It's true that the greatest threat to America's security and prosperity comes not from the damage that terrorists can inflict on us, but the damage that terrorism can persuade us to inflict on ourselves. One way of avoiding that problem is through effective counterterrorism operations overseas. Isolationism appeals to every instinct we have to cut our risks and maximize our benefits, but it is dangerously naïve to believe that the world will simply leave us alone. No country can do more than America to lead an international fight against terrorism, and it must be done.

Islamic State militants in Iraq and Syria can threaten the stability of the entire Middle East and could eventually promote terrorist attacks inside America and Europe. Washington can't continue to ignore this region's small problems until they turn into big ones. The United States can and should lead an international effort to ensure that ISIS remains isolated, even if it can't immediately be dismantled and destroyed. That doesn't mean U.S. ground forces in Iraq. This commitment will depend as much on Washington's ability to coordinate the efforts of others as on U.S. firepower. U.S. ties with Saudi Arabia will be crucial for this struggle, because the Saudis are the only existing power with an interest in seeing ISIS survive.

In addition, according to credible press reports, U.S. Special Operations now uses African air bases in Burkina Faso, South Sudan, Kenya, Uganda, Djibouti, and the Seychelles to gather information on and target al-Qaeda-inspired militant groups in Mali, Niger, Yemen, Somalia, Nigeria, the Democratic Republic of Congo, the Central African Republic, and Sudan.[17] That's necessary, because al-Qaeda affiliates like Somalia's al-Shabaab, Nigeria's Boko Haram, and Yemen's al-Qaeda in the Arabian Peninsula couldn't care less about the U.S. government's respect for the civil liberties of American citizens. They want to strike Western targets—and the al-Qaeda core that inspired them is still targeting the United States.

Use Drones

The U.S. military should use drones, because they offer a low-cost, low-risk method of killing those who would kill Americans. It's true that drones also kill civilians. A Moneyball approach to foreign policy is not intended to relieve America's elected leaders or military commanders of the moral responsibility for taking extraordinary steps to reduce the risk that our actions kill innocent men, women, and children. We must also acknowledge, however, that wherever there is conflict, innocent people die, whether the weapons that steal their lives are ancient or remotely controlled. In that respect, drones are no different from any other weapon in the American arsenal.

It's true that drones emasculate those who govern the countries they strike, undermining our relations with governments that are not our enemies. But state officials in Pakistan, Afghanistan, Yemen, and Somalia know that they are at greater risk than Americans from those targeted for automated attacks. Some argue that the use of drones violates international law. If you oppose their use on that basis, then you must also oppose the manned attack that killed Osama bin Laden, an assault that also violated Pakistan's territorial integrity. In that case, you value the sanctity of Pakistani airspace more than the opportunity to kill the world's most accomplished terrorist. That's a legitimate moral position. But leaders faced with imminent threats must often choose among options that are terrible each in its own way, and it is immoral to ignore that reality. It is also immoral to condemn a leader's choice without offering an honest, well-considered alternative.

Those who champion a so-called Independent America will tell you that drones create more enemies than they kill, and that America will attract more admirers by perfecting American democracy. Do you really believe that young men living among the tribes of the Afghan-Pakistan border are less likely to support extremist ideologies if we build better schools in Ohio and better hospitals in Arkansas? Do you accept that Somali jihadis are less likely to plan attacks on Western targets or that U.S. embassies around the world will be safer if U.S. policymakers redouble their commitment to American civil liberties? In the real world, a leader must often choose the least bad of many bad options. Drones achieve military objectives with much less risk for our military and at much lower cost to our economy. Use them.

Never Walk Alone

In one sense, the Russian intervention in Ukraine did Moneyball America a big favor: It persuaded many reluctant Europeans (and Americans) that NATO still has a purpose and is worth the investment. NATO states can do more together than any of its individual members—including the United States—can do alone. NATO skeptics in America should drop their insistence that Washington act without the constraints imposed by its friends, because the alliance allows the United States to share dangers and burdens with willing, able, and like-minded partners. That's good for the American soldier and for the American taxpayer.

And, yes, wherever possible, America's leaders should "lead from behind." Barack Obama didn't coin that phrase; an anonymous Obama adviser used it during an interview with a journal-ist.[18] But in some cases, leading from behind can help future U.S. presidents manage the risks and costs of conflict. In Libya in 2011, fourteen NATO members and four partner countries prevented Muammar Qaddafi from carrying out a promise to slaughter tens of thousands of his own people—and then they removed him from power. France, Britain, Italy, Canada, Denmark, Norway, Belgium, and others struck 90 percent of all NATO targets. Spain, the Neth-erlands, Turkey, Greece, and Romania enforced an arms embargo at sea. Sweden, not a NATO member, contributed naval and air force personnel and equipment. The United Arab Emirates, Qatar, Jordan, and Morocco also contributed.[19] There was not a single U.S. casualty.[20]

The point is not that Washington should persuade others to do all the heavy lifting. NATO jets were able to hit their targets only because U.S. cruise missiles had already wiped out Libya's air de-fenses. When Europeans ran short on precision-guided missiles, Washington sent them more.[21] Without the United States, there would have been no mission. Critics carp that while NATO rid the world of a dangerous monster, it hasn't created a stable Libya. That charge misses the point. From a Moneyball perspective, the goal was not to bomb Libya into democracy, start a war, or launch an-other improvisational bout of nation-building. It was to give Liby-ans a chance to escape the fate Qaddafi intended for them, and to enable them to begin the long-term process of building their own future. Libyans will have to build the next Libya.

Libya was an exceptional case. Syria, for example, is not so easy to bomb without killing large numbers of civilians, and the fallout could destabilize much of the Middle East. An attack on Bashar al-Assad might also have put a permanent hold on negotiation over Iran's nuclear program, a matter of far greater importance for U.S.

interests. But wherever possible, America's president must resist school yard demands to talk and act tough at all times. In select cases, leading from behind is a Moneyball-friendly formula for success. From in front or from behind, only America could have led such an operation. It needed to be done in Libya, and a similar use of NATO force will be needed somewhere else one day soon.

Negotiate—Especially with Enemies

A Moneyball approach demands a more modest and realistic foreign policy, one that respects the core interests of other powerful states. Isolationists, both liberals and conservatives, reject the need to sometimes talk with tyrants, and a handshake with Fidel Castro or a smile with Iran's president draws fire from across the political spectrum. Saudi Arabia is a family-owned business with a human rights record that is even more appalling than we know. Yet we buy Saudi oil because without it the U.S. economy won't create the jobs that allow millions of Americans to feed their families and educate their children. We buy Saudi oil because it allows the U.S. economy to generate the wealth that pays the salaries of schoolteachers, police officers, firefighters, and our military. We buy Saudi oil because we still need it. The real world is a complicated place, and it's naïve to think we can protect America without sometimes working with governments whose values we don't like.

Presidents Richard Nixon and Ronald Reagan had little in common beyond their affiliation with the Republican Party. But America won the Cold War in part because Nixon was willing to sit down and do business with Chinese leader Mao Tse-tung, one of the twentieth century's most notorious despots, and because Reagan had the moral intelligence to spot an opportunity for sincere engagement in Soviet leader Mikhail Gorbachev's opening to the West. If, before leaving office, President Obama is able to exploit new opportunities to promote greater openness in Iran and Cuba, this will be among his finest accomplishments. If the next U.S. president will extend the efforts of Jimmy Carter, Ronald Reagan, George H. W. Bush, Bill Clinton, George W. Bush, and Barack Obama to engage China, he or she will be acting in America's interest.

Americans believe their country has a legitimate sphere of influence. It is neither immoral nor cowardly to acknowledge that other powers have them too. That's why the expansion of NATO into Russia's backyard amounted to an unnecessary provocation of Moscow at its most vulnerable moment—and why we must be careful to ensure that our pivot to Asia does not become a Cold War–minded bid to contain China's legitimate aspirations for greater regional and international influence.

Remain Flexible

Flexibility is another critical element of a successful Moneyball foreign policy and another means of managing costs. U.S. policymakers too often create strategically rigid tests for themselves that can only be passed by accepting new risks and burdens where the costs outweigh the benefits. America fought in Vietnam because the domino theory determined that we must fight just about anything that appeared to be communist aggression, whenever and wherever it appeared. That assumption led us to see threats to U.S. national security where none existed. U.S. forces invaded Iraq in 2003 because President Bush determined that if sanctions could not force regime change, the military must. In this case, shrugging off Saddam's bravado and keeping him isolated was the better choice. In 2013, when Syria's Bashar al-Assad appeared ready to use chemical weapons on his own people, President Obama drew a red line. Assad's use of these weapons, Obama warned, was a "game-changer." Assad is then believed to have used those chemical weapons, but Washington took no action against his government, instead allowing Russia to broker a hasty deal to destroy the weapons. Obama chose flexibility; he was wise to do nothing. His mistake was in drawing a red line that he was not prepared to enforce.

Use Sanctions

Sanctions are another foreign policy tool that can be effective in the right circumstances—and they will always be cheaper than war. Over time, they forced the leaders of apartheid South Africa to acknowledge the need to accept genuine democracy in that country. They prevented Saddam Hussein from banking the money necessary to develop the dangerous arsenal of weapons that would have made him a much greater threat to the Middle East and the world. Sanctions (and the U.S. invasion of Iraq, let's be fair) helped persuade Muammar Qaddafi to give up his own nuclear material. The impact of sanctions, tightened significantly under President Obama, on Iran's economy brought that country back to the nuclear bargaining table.

Unfortunately, as Fidel Castro would be happy to remind us, sanctions sometimes accomplish nothing of value. The United States should have enough experience with sanctions to know where they will never work. Restrictions that spread the pain across an entire population can never undermine North Korea, because North Korea's leaders don't care if their people starve, and they need international isolation to keep their grip on power. Even those penalties intended to target the elite, by freezing foreign bank accounts and denying them imported luxury goods, will probably never produce positive results. Efforts to sanction North Korean banks, for example, simply make life even more miserable for North Korea's people, without having any impact on the ruling Kim family and its elite enablers, because it complicates the efforts of foreign NGOs to provide North Koreans with relief from illness and hunger.[22]

Yet in some cases sanctions can be a necessary tool even when they can't, by themselves, get us what we want. Visa restrictions and asset freezes on Putin's personal friends would never have changed his choices in Ukraine. Central to his personal vision of Russia is the creation of a Eurasian Union, a reconstituted Russian Empire that will prove Russian exceptionalism once and for all by creating a counterweight to the European Union. Without Ukraine, once an industrial powerhouse and the agricultural heartland of the Soviet Union, there is no Russian Empire. Even sanctions that helped push Russia into recession could not persuade Putin to sing a different tune. But a Moneyball approach suggests that sanctions can offer a cost-effective way to raise the costs for those who threaten the stability of a strategically important region. In particular, the United States continues to exercise enormous influence over the global financial sector. Imposing penalties on foreign banks, denying them access to financial markets, can be a ruthlessly effective (and cost-effective) way of applying economic and political pressure on a vulnerable government. The United States should not consider going to war with Russia over Ukraine—though a Russian attack on a NATO member is a completely different story—but sanctions, including on the Russian banking sector, offer some means of ensuring that Putin knows he will feel the pain of every action that we don't like.

Use American Energy

Fortunately, the architects of American foreign policy also have more benign tools at their disposal. It won't be obvious as you count the U.S. battleships protecting traffic in the Strait of Hormuz, but America's energy revolution will move global markets and change international politics in years to come. The effects of this change will take time, but they are likely to last. A drive toward energy self-sufficiency will bring welcome news for the long-term health of America's economy, and a Moneyball approach to foreign policy should lead U.S. policymakers to allow for the export of significant quantities of some of these new energy reserves to improve ties with key allies.

That will take time and hard work, because the U.S. government is not yet well organized to use energy policy to advance the country's geopolitical interests. The U.S. Department of Energy is not as directly involved in the formulation of foreign and security policy as governments in energy-exporting countries like Saudi Arabia and Russia—or other major importers like Japan, China, or Germany. Nor should we forget that traditional mistrust of government interference in commerce ensures that Washington is not very effective at crafting industrial policy. U.S. refiners, manufacturers, and consumer groups will resist efforts to boost energy exports, because they want to maximize the benefits of cheap energy for the domestic economy—though Putin's actions in Ukraine boost Moneyball America here as well, by persuading otherwise reluctant lawmakers that if rogues use energy as a weapon, we should too.

The primary responsibility of an effective energy policy in an energy-importing country like the United States is to ensure that we have enough energy to heat our homes, fuel our cars, and boost our economy. Once these needs are met, however, Washington can and should export significant volumes of liquefied natural gas (LNG). Our government doesn't own these assets, and energy companies will sell them at the highest price. But even if most of our energy exports are headed for Asia, the increase in supply will help our European friends and allies satisfy their growing energy needs at a reasonable cost, indirectly easing their reliance on Russia. Though neighbors like Ukraine and Poland remain deeply dependent on Gazprom, Russia's gas monopoly, for affordable natural gas supplies, each appears to have enough shale gas deposits of its own to sharply reduce Russia's leverage with their governments. Washington can help. The U.S. government has created a program to transfer unconventional gas technologies to friendly countries like Poland and Ukraine.

Guarantees on LNG exports will also be written into the Trans-Pacific Partnership, a U.S. foreign policy priority, enhancing Washington's leverage with negotiating partners by helping them meet their energy needs. More on that crucial agreement below. The rise of China and the anxiety it generates in Japan have given Washington and Tokyo good reason to reaffirm and deepen their long-term alliance, and U.S. energy exports to Japan can help. Japan is already the world's leading importer of LNG, and its imports from the Middle East and North Africa are much more expensive than the price enjoyed in the United States.[23] Japan will also profit from reliable energy supplies from a predictable partner. The United States will benefit by expanding its commercial and security partnership with a traditional ally that can provide a long-term foothold in the region that is most important for the future of the global economy.

As noted, to build a stable and sustainable geopolitical balance in Asia, better and deeper U.S. relations with Tokyo demand better and deeper U.S. relations with Beijing. The U.S. energy revolution can help here too. China has every incentive to develop its domestic energy potential. Though the United States is becoming less dependent on the always volatile Middle East, China is becoming more reliant on that region's energy producers, some of which generate more than their share of political turmoil. China is believed to have larger deposits of shale gas even than the United States, yet lacks the technology and know-how needed to exploit them.[24] Cooperation on such an important project won't come easily, but given the stakes for both sides, it's a path worth exploring. By helping China develop this resource, the United States can enhance the relationship most important for global peace and prosperity over the next quarter century.

American Prosperity

It is not America's job to make the world safe for democracy, but we would be wise to actively promote the trade and investment needed to establish a stabilizing international economic interdependence. President Obama has tried to move U.S. security policy toward a focus on making the country more secure by making it more prosperous. With that in mind, Secretary of State Hillary Clinton laid the groundwork for "economic statecraft," an approach guided by awareness that expanded trade and investment ties have never been more important for national strength and resilience.

The next president must translate this vision into policies that extend U.S. influence abroad and spur economic growth at home. Here is where the Trans-Pacific Partnership (TPP) looms large. Global trade talks can't produce the results we want, as the stalled World Trade Organization's Doha trade round has vividly demonstrated. Too many negotiators at the table and the domestic political demands of too many governments produce lowest-common-denominator results. Instead, the future lies with regional agreements of unprecedented scale.

There are two reasons why TPP is so important. First, trade will be crucial for future U.S. growth, and this deal is as big as they come. Negotiations now include the United States, Canada, Mexico, Chile, Peru, Australia, New Zealand, Vietnam, Singapore, Malaysia, and Brunei. With Japan, the group represents roughly one-third of world trade and 40 percent of global GDP.[25] It's a geostrategic game-changer and a crucial component of a Moneyball U.S. foreign policy.

Second, TPP is the right answer to China's state-driven economic model. China's rise has created important challenges for the United States and its economy, in particular by empowering a system of state capitalism that gives political officials a powerful role in directing market activity. By using state-owned companies, state-run banks, and privately owned but politically reliable national champion firms to achieve political goals, China has made it much more difficult for U.S. and other foreign companies to compete on a level playing field. TPP can help counter the growth of Chinese-style state capitalism and extend U.S. influence in the Pacific in much the same way that potential European Union membership once encouraged reform in former Warsaw Pact countries, states that might otherwise have followed a familiar path of least resistance back toward state-run economics and authoritarian rule.

This trade pact is not an attempt to contain China or stunt its growth. Instead, it's a big investment in the future of free markets—and an invitation to China's neighbors to share the benefits of free trade while deepening their political and security relationships with Washington. It's also a signal that America intends to remain in Asia as a stabilizing force, even as China becomes a more influential economic and security player in the region and beyond.

Washington will have to compromise on key provisions of the deal, but TPP will provide the United States with something it badly needs: a lasting achievement for liberal trade, investment, and regulatory principles in the world's most economically promising region, one that might otherwise become frozen in China's lengthening state capitalist shadow. With a similarly ambitious agreement, known as the Transatlantic Trade and Investment Partnership (TTIP), already in the works with the European Union, America's next president has a golden opportunity to reshape the global trade and investment landscape to better serve U.S. interests and enhance growth prospects at home.

Perhaps the best reason to do these things is that they are doable. On questions of budgets and borrowing, immigration reform, gun control, and a dozen other hot topics, Democrats and Republicans continue to stand miles apart. But if the next president will devote time, energy, and political capital to a trade deal that defines the United States as a permanent Pacific power and tightens the bonds that bind America and its allies, he or she will have enough votes from the two parties—and the support of U.S. business leaders—to make it happen.

Let the twenty-first-century arms race become a trade race.

Today, Communist China enjoys higher trade volumes than America with 124 countries, while free-trade America's trade outstrips China's with just 76. In total trade volume, China surpassed the United States in 2012 to become the world's number one trading nation. Let this setback become our "Sputnik moment," the point at which we accept that we have fallen behind in a race we can't afford to lose, that a serious new commitment is required, that we must draw on the best American traditions of commerce and creativity, and that we must act. The world's governments don't agree on democracy, but even autocracies like China and Russia have invested in the power of markets to power their prosperity. There is no more effective means of providing all the world's governments with a stake in a stable and prosperous world than to forge an elaborate web of new trade and investment agreements.

Those who oppose trade will remind us of the extensive trade flows among major European powers on the eve of World War I, and that in the decade before World War II the United States was both the leading importer of Japanese exports and the leading source of that country's raw materials.[26] But this criticism ignores two critical factors. First, the world's great powers are no longer governed by leaders who believe they must conquer new territory to find the resources needed to fuel an industrial economy.[27] Second, according to historian Richard Rosecrance, "about 90 percent of foreign investment in 1913 was portfolio investment, that is, it represented small holdings of foreign shares that could easily be disposed of on the stock exchange. Direct investment, that which represents more than a 10 percent share of the total ownership of a foreign firm, was only one tenth of the total."[28]

In that respect, the world has changed dramatically. In developing countries, those most prone to internal and external conflict and where investment is most needed, yearly foreign direct investment (FDI) inflows have increased from an average of less than $10 billion in the 1970s to more than $700 billion in 2012. For the first time ever in 2012, developing economies absorbed more FDI than did developed countries, attracting 52 percent of global FDI flows. More remarkable is the fact that developing economies' FDI *out*flows, the investments these countries make in other countries, reached $468 billion in 2014, a record 34.6 percent of the global total, according to the UN Conference on Trade and Development.[29]

By itself, the economic interdependence created by rising levels of trade and direct investment can never eliminate the risk of war. But by giving as many countries as possible as great a share as possible in the stability and prosperity of other countries, war becomes costlier and, on balance, less likely. That's good for the American soldier, American consumer, and American taxpayer. And that's Moneyball.

Finally, a Moneyball foreign policy guides us to set aside national vanity to find the wisdom and humility to accept that China has something to teach us about trade and investment, and nowhere is that lesson more obvious than in Africa. Across this rising continent, the new American theme must be investment and trade, not aid. For decades, the United States has offered humanitarian handouts to African governments but has not invested in the infrastructure—the roads, bridges, and port facilities—that Africa needs to realize its considerable economic potential. China doesn't invest in Africa to democratize the continent or to build the institutions needed to improve rule of law or entrench respect for human rights. They invest to ensure that China receives the oil, gas, metals, and minerals needed to fuel its economy and create jobs, and to profit Chinese companies, many of them owned by the state.

Washington should follow Beijing's lead, but we can also learn from its mistakes. Chinese companies too often bring Chinese workers to construct the projects they bankroll. American companies should instead create jobs for local workers. Investment in Africa represents an opportunity, not a moral responsibility. A Moneyball approach demands that we invest for profit, not charity. Africa too will reap the rewards.

Costs and Benefits

Why should the architects of U.S. foreign policy play Moneyball? Because everyone else is. Unlike the Oakland A's, our challenge is that everyone but us is already playing this more rational game. Beijing isn't spending more on its military, cutting new trade deals, and extending its influence in order to export Chinese values, remake the world in China's image, or provide global public goods. It's doing these things to make China stronger, safer, and more prosperous. Here too we should follow China's example. Some U.S. actions, like securing free passage for tanker traffic through the Strait of Hormuz, will have global benefits. But that's not why America should take them. We should do these things because they serve U.S. interests. Moneyball values are the product of solid American thrift and common sense.

Isolationists argue that America should never accept costs and risks that don't pay quick and apparent dividends. That's foolish. To build a Moneyball American foreign policy, it is less important that our leaders spend less than that they spend wisely. With that in mind, there is no finer historical example of Moneyball America than the shrewd investment calculation known as the Marshall Plan, an idea that an isolationist president or congressional leadership would have strangled at birth.

To safeguard the hard-won peace at the end of World War II, President Harry Truman understood that new international institutions like the United Nations and the World Bank were not enough. America needed an aggressive plan to help rebuild Europe and its economies. In 1947, the United States imported just half of what it exported across the Atlantic. Without an unprecedented infusion of funds, Truman feared, Europeans would run out of money, the Soviets would extend their influence into Western Europe, and Americans would lose their most reliable important allies and trade partners.[30]

Many Americans have forgotten, or have never read about, the challenges and threats facing Western Europe just after the war. Soviet troops tightened the Kremlin's grip on Eastern Europe, and communist governments began to appear. In Western Europe, economic despair and an infusion of Marxist ideology began to take hold. Local communist parties made major gains in France and Italy. To protect friendly governments, bolster historically lucrative export markets, and counter the expansion of communist influence, Truman moved to bankroll European reconstruction on an unprecedented scale. He also had the wisdom and modesty to recognize that congressional support for the plan, particularly from postwar isolationists bent on repeating the mistakes of the 1920s, depended on naming it for popular general George Marshall rather than for himself.

In its first year, the price tag for the Marshall Plan amounted to a full 10 percent of the U.S. federal budget, but over time this investment paid historic dividends.[31] By 1952, Western European economies were already operating at double their prewar levels.[32] Washington's decision to keep troops in Europe provided a security umbrella that allowed Western European governments to focus their spending on domestic economic development. The Marshall Plan remains the wisest investment in American foreign policy history. By Cold War standards, this was a milestone of rational, cold-blooded cost-benefit analysis.

Truman's presidency provides another Moneyball lesson. Eisenhower was still in uniform when Truman made clear that American foreign policy is made by civilians. Those who argue for Independent America are right that we must guard against the risk that our foreign policy will fall into the hands of military hawks or crusaders driven by neoconservative nonsense. In other words, if

Harry Truman knew which general to immortalize, he also knew which one to fire.

Fighting the Korean War might have prevented other Cold War conflicts, including perhaps in Japan. But Douglas MacArthur intended to expand the conflict in Korea into China, bringing Moscow and Beijing into alignment as nothing else could. Some will argue that America had an obligation to free China of communism just as it helped free Europe of fascism and Japan of militarism. But World War III would have cost much more—for Americans and for the world—than the Marshall Plan. Even if the United States had won an unqualified victory over Communist China, wouldn't the U.S. military then have been forced to occupy the much larger China as it occupied Japan? What would that have cost? Would it have worked? Truman, like the elder President Bush, knew when to stop. Douglas MacArthur, like the younger President Bush, did not.

* * * * * *

Let's be clear: America is *not* an exceptional nation. America is the most powerful, but that doesn't mean it's always right. We are not all-knowing, and the universal benefit is never our main concern. America has done much good in the world, and it will do more. But it has also done a lot of damage, particularly by trying to force our values on others without careful consideration of the consequences. Those who make American foreign policy and those who implement it must be guided by both discretion and humility. And they must remember that freedom is in the eye of the beholder.

As you listen to the next round of presidential debates, imagine you're listening to Chinese political leaders telling their people that they are the world's strongest, best, and brightest—that China, not America, is the best hope for a peaceful future. Imagine the French president telling his people that only France can offer the world a true moral compass. Imagine listening to Vladimir Putin telling his people that God has a special purpose for Russia. If you can imagine hearing these words from the leaders of other countries, then you can understand the reactions of their citizens to American debates on American exceptionalism. As George Bernard Shaw once wrote, "Patriotism is, fundamentally, a conviction that a particular country is the best in the world because you were born in it." We may believe that ours is the most virtuous great power in history, and that people around the world are inspired by our example. But we can also accept that many are sick of sermons from our flag-lapel-wearing leaders—and that they resent our reflexive grandstanding. We can't expect others to love their countries less or feel less loyalty for their homelands as we work to persuade them that our ideas are best.[33]

It's time to cast a vote for strength, not the appearance of strength. Vote for American thrift, modesty, discretion, and sound judgment—the attributes that made the United States the most powerful and influential nation on earth. Vote for a foreign policy written not in poetry but in prose, one that will enhance our security and prosperity in the world we actually live, not the one we wish for. We can't afford to hide from the world, but nor can we force our values on everyone else. Vote for the best traditions of our past.

Vote Moneyball.

Let's return to the quiz. Here is how a champion of Moneyball America might answer (in italics with a brief explanation for that choice).

A Moneyball America Answer Key

1. Freedom is:

    a. The right of every human being.

    b. Fragile. Americans must protect it right here at home.

    c. *In the eye of the beholder.*

What gives us the right to define another country's values?

2. America is:

    a. Exceptional because of what it represents.

    b. Exceptional because of all it has done for the world.

    c. *Not an exceptional nation. America is the most powerful, but that doesn't mean it's always right.*

Our country is in trouble if we can't speak frankly about its shortcomings alongside its great strengths.

3. Which of these statements best expresses your opinion?

    a. America will be better off if we mind our own business and let other countries get along the best they can.

    b. America must lead.

c. *The primary purpose of U.S. foreign policy should be to make America safer and more prosperous.*

Our resources are limited. We can't solve every problem, but nor can we hide from those challenges that can compromise our security and prosperity.

4. China is:

   a. *America's greatest challenge and greatest opportunity.*

   b. The place where too many American jobs have gone.

   c. The world's largest dictatorship.

We can't tell China what to do, but nor can we ignore it. We must both engage China and hedge our bets on its future.

5. America's biggest problem in the Middle East is that:

   a. Washington supports the region's dictators rather than its people.

   b. *Washington ignores small problems until they turn into big ones.*

   c. Washington believes it can manage an unmanageable region.

Respond to fires before they burn out of control.

6. U.S. spy capabilities:

   a. *Will always be a double-edged sword.*

   b. Threaten our privacy.

c. Are vital for protecting America.

Powerful states have always spied on one another and always will, but we must use this tool only when and where it can make America more secure.

7. The primary responsibility of the president of the United States is:

   a. To advance U.S. interests at home and abroad.

   b. To promote, protect, and defend the Constitution of the United States.

   c. To lead.

We hire presidents to add value, not to lead crusades.

8. Which of the following best expresses your view?

   a. A great leader can change the world.

   b. A great leader must lead by example.

   c. In the real world, any leader must often choose the least bad of many bad options.

A president must have the courage to cope with the problems that cannot be solved.

9. Which is the most at risk?

   a. America's economy.

   b. America's international reputation.

    c. The respect of our leaders for America's founding principles.

If we build a foreign policy that saps our economic strength, our power and prosperity cannot last.

10. I hope that by the year 2050:

    a. *America will share the burdens of leadership with reliable, like-minded allies.*

    b. Americans will have created a more perfect union at home.

    c. American leadership will have helped as many people as possible around the world topple the tyrants who deny them the freedom they deserve.

We will always need friends to help us do the things that must be done.

CHAPTER 5

Indispensable America

Leadership—for America and for the World

The reasonable man adapts himself to the world: the
unreasonable one persists in trying to adapt the world to himself.
Therefore all progress depends on the unreasonable man.
—George Bernard Shaw,
Maxims for Revolutionists

Yes, everyone else is playing Moneyball. That is precisely why America must do more.

Those who believe that Americans can simply ignore every potentially costly conflict, or that our leaders will ever have the luxury of picking and choosing their challenges, don't understand our interconnected world. Today's threats surge across stock markets, hurtle through cyberspace, and can cross borders in a single suitcase. We will be safer only if others live in peace. We will remain prosperous only if other countries produce middle classes that can afford to buy the products we make. We need allies and partners that are strong and stable. We need poorer nations to prevent terrorists and criminals from using ungoverned corners of their territory as safe havens. In short, Americans can only be more secure in a world where democracy, rule of law, access to information, freedom of speech, and human rights are *universally* recognized and protected, because these values create lasting strength, resilience, security, and wealth in the societies that establish and protect them.

Only America can promote and protect these values on a global scale. Europeans honor them, but without U.S. leadership, twenty-eight EU governments and complex European institutions with limited mandates won't persuade reluctant citizens to accept the burdens that come with consistent global leadership.* No one else will fill this breach. Democracies like Japan and India have an important role to play, but they won't project global strength anytime soon. Don't look to China and Russia. Their leaders know that an embrace of these freedoms would loosen their grip on power.

Americans say we believe in these values, and that ours is an exceptional nation because we have given so much to advance them. Others are tired of hearing that, and some Americans don't want the responsibilities that come with this role. But like it or not, America *is* exceptional. For all its faults and mistakes, the United States has done more than any nation in history to ensure that leaders in other countries must answer to their citizens. It provided a winning alternative to fascism and communism when the world needed one. It created the institutions and innovations that have helped lift hundreds of millions of people out of poverty. It has offered hope and opportunity to a historically unprecedented number

---

* This is especially true given the European Union's unpopularity with many Europeans.

of those seeking a better life, and has set a standard of individual freedom and opportunity against which people everywhere measure their own governments.

This work is not finished. While other governments play Moneyball, someone must bolster the resilience of our open international economic system and promote balanced and sustainable global growth. Someone must lead the alliances that manage conflict, prevent terrorists from gaining access to the world's most dangerous weapons, contain threats in cyberspace, and fight transnational crime and the worst effects of climate change. There can be no lasting security and prosperity anywhere if these things are not done. Who but America can do them? Who but America can lead?

We must rebuild the foundation of American power—military, economic, and political. We must modernize our traditional alliances and form new ones, not by asking new partners to serve our interests but by actively seeking out new opportunities for mutually profitable exchange. It is not enough to have the world's most powerful military; we must prepare for a new generation of asymmetric threats and aggressively strengthen our partners on the front lines of the ongoing war with Islamic militants. America must again become the world's lead trading nation.[1] We must shape an international order that ensures that prosperity is shared, in part by leading the effort to enforce the rules that protect security and commerce. We must invest in systems that protect global health and manage responses to humanitarian crises.

The complexity of today's international order demands a strategy. Independent America is not a strategy but a refusal to create one. Moneyball is not a strategy; it's a set of tactics designed, on the fly and on the cheap, to keep inconvenient foreign policy challenges at arm's length. America can't avoid the rest of the world. We can't simply cope with threats as they emerge. We must help shape the global order. This is not the moment to think small. Americans must now think bigger and in more ambitious terms than at any previous moment in our history.

What purpose should America serve in the twenty-first century? We must move creatively, patiently, and wisely to ensure that *every nation on earth will become a democracy*. To ensure that every country will be governed by laws that protect not just the stability of the state but the rights of the individual. That every country must establish and protect freedoms of religion, speech, assembly, and the press—and build an economic system governed by internationally recognized rules of trade and investment. We must do these things because freedom is the right of every human being.

This is not a call to use our military to topple all the world's tyrants. We will never have the power to do that. Instead, we must use every tool at our disposal—military, economic, financial, political, and cultural—to help enable the citizens of every nation to create their own irresistible momentum for change and topple the tyrants who deny them the freedom they deserve. In some countries, this process will take years. In others, it will take decades. But we must see beyond the need for results that become visible within a single presidency toward the achievement of one of the few commitments on which Democrats and Republicans wholeheartedly agree: support for liberty.

Sound unreasonable? It's unreasonable to believe that if we hide from the rest of the world, tomorrow's problems will respect our neutrality and leave us alone. It's unreasonable to believe in some carefully calibrated Moneyball-inspired notion that presidents can choose which challenges to accept and which to ignore. And though our investment in universal political and economic freedom can't be fully realized in the next ten years or twenty-five years, it is never unreasonable to make long-term investments in the values we say we believe in.

This is not a call to return to a past that never was. We must build an entirely new American foreign policy, one dedicated to the proposition that freedom will make us, and everyone else, stronger, more secure, and more prosperous—if only we have the patience, wisdom, and courage to act on our beliefs. The primary responsibility of our elected leaders has always been to safeguard our security and help promote a general prosperity. That will never change. But as a people, is that all we aspire to? The United States has answered the call again and again and again. The time has come to become a truly indispensable nation.

With the opportunity to answer a higher calling, why should America do less?

Begin at Home

Let's start with those issues the Independent America advocates are right about. Our leaders must do all they can within the letter and spirit of our Constitution to prevent another terrorist attack on U.S. soil. The primary responsibility of our government is to protect the homeland, and we must make the necessary investment in the security of our borders, ports, airports, electrical grid, nuclear facilities, financial system, and other critical infrastructure.

We must also bolster the strength of the U.S. economy, the engine of American power. Only a dynamic and resilient economy can finance the state-of-the-art twenty-first-century military that Americans deserve. Without it, we can't use trade and investment as effective tools of foreign policy. Most important, without an economy that creates jobs and opportunity, our elected leaders can't rebuild and maintain the public support necessary for an ambitious foreign policy.

We must make a more serious effort to reduce our national debt. The dollar remains strong, helping America avoid the risk of a debt crisis. Yet the inevitable, gradual erosion of its status as the world's dominant reserve currency ensures that our leaders must take extraordinary steps to substantially reduce U.S. debt. Some argue for raising the age at which Americans qualify for Social Security and Medicare. Others favor something called "graduated eligibility," an approach that would raise the age of eligibility only for those deemed wealthy enough to wait. Still others call for changes to the way in which benefit amounts are calculated.* There may be many other ways to make substantive progress toward reforming our entitlement system and reducing our national debt. But the American people deserve to see Democrats and Republicans work toward an intelligent compromise that will boost foreign and domestic confidence in the U.S. economy's lasting strength.

Champions of Independent or Moneyball America are also right that Americans must continue to invest in our people and their future by revitalizing our education system, a plan that will require creative thinking, political will, and considerable financial commitment. We must continue to devote the resources toward research and development needed to ensure that America's economy remains the world's most innovative. Even as we produce more hydrocarbon energy at home, we must continue to diversify our fuel mix to minimize our national dependence on any one form of energy and any single source of supply, even a domestic one.

---

* For a more detailed explanation of some of these ideas, see Andrew Sullivan, "Will Obama Raise the Medicare Eligibility Age?" *The Dish,* December 10, 2012, http://dish.andrewsullivan .com/2012/12/10/will-obama-raise-the-medicare-eligibility-age/.

Beware False Choices

Yet those who insist that we can afford to invest at home only if we renounce our international leadership miss the essential point: Fulfilling our responsibilities abroad is crucial for our own prosperity, because in a globalized world we can't succeed unless others succeed too. We need confident commercial partners with whom to trade. We need others to help finance our success by investing in our debt. We must ensure that U.S. companies that create jobs at home by building market share abroad can operate within a safe and stable international environment. We must help ensure the free flow of trade and vital commodities like oil, gas, metals, and minerals, not just through the Strait of Hormuz but everywhere our economic interests are at stake. And not just to protect our own economic interests but those of the entire global economy on which our interests will increasingly depend.

Global economic interdependence is a fact of life. During the Cold War, peace between the U.S. and the USSR depended on "mutually assured destruction," the certain knowledge in both Moscow and Washington that a nuclear attack by one side would trigger immediate retaliation by the other. Today, that shared vulnerability is economic—and it is global. In 2008, a financial crisis in the United States pushed most of the world into recession. It forced China's leaders to spend hundreds of billions of dollars to create enough jobs at home to ensure that they could maintain the stability of China's economy and of the country itself.[2] Without a well-coordinated international response to bolster buckling institutions in America and Europe, it could have been worse.

Just as China is profoundly vulnerable to economic conditions in the United States, so Americans are exposed to the impact of change inside China, which one day soon will have the world's largest economy. A market meltdown in China would trigger a tsunami that crashes ashore in nearly every country in the world. Other governments would do their best to coordinate an emergency response, but China's less mature political and financial institutions are likely to prove much less sturdy—and much harder to rescue—than the Western banks that needed help in 2008 and 2009.

Where might a Chinese meltdown come from? Most likely from internal stresses within China itself. But it might also come from an external conflict—a trade war or even a military confrontation—that pits China against one of its neighbors, for example, or an international crisis that triggers a spike in world energy prices. Washington can and should do everything possible to help minimize these risks to manage the immediate and lasting fallout for both the U.S. and global economies. It is foolish and dangerous to believe that we can ignore this problem and focus only on challenges within our borders.

China's potential fragility is hardly the only source of risk from abroad that threatens us at home. In fact, there is no greater threat to America's future than a terrorist with a nuclear weapon. That's why the Nuclear Non-Proliferation Treaty (NPT) is so important. The United States cannot allow rogue states like Iran to develop nuclear weapons, not just because Iran is a potentially dangerous regional player, but because an Iranian bomb might well trigger a Middle East arms race that makes nuclear weapons and materiel widely enough available to fall easily into the hands of a terrorist who cares nothing about mutually assured destruction. The United States must ensure that this does not happen.

For those who have signed the NPT, the incentive to cheat on the agreement is high. After all, a state armed with a nuclear weapon faces virtually no risk of invasion. Enforcement of such a sensitive international treaty demands economic strength, extraordinary diplomatic influence, and considerable military power. America can't enforce the NPT alone. If it could, Pakistan and North Korea wouldn't have nuclear weapons. But without U.S. leadership, backed by American influence, money, and muscle, there would be no NPT, and we would all be living in a more dangerous world.

Beyond the nuclear risk is the day-to-day business of fighting terrorism. It is no longer news that we live in a world where a failed state halfway around the world threatens U.S. national security. Afghanistan will matter for America long after the last U.S. troops have come home. As long as ISIS holds ground in Iraq and Syria, those countries will remain priority concerns for U.S. policymakers. As terrorist training grounds, Libya, Mali, Nigeria, Yemen, and Somalia all matter—for their neighbors and for the world. It's true that when we kill terrorists in faraway places, we increase the risk that new terrorists will step forward. But we can't avoid that risk by hiding at home. We must continue to try to deny terrorists safe haven inside other countries. We must disrupt and dismantle terror cells wherever they exist. We must strengthen our vulnerable allies and coordinate the sharing of information among governments. These commitments demand a global strategy, one that only America has the means to direct.

This is also a world in which one country's public health crisis can quickly become everybody's business. In 2002–2003, an outbreak of severe acute respiratory syndrome in southern China killed more than 700 people and spread to more than two dozen countries.[3] H5N1 avian influenza, better known as bird flu, unexpectedly infected nearly 650 people in fifteen countries a decade ago.[4] As of this writing, the Ebola outbreak of 2014–15 has killed more than 11,000 people.[5] The risk is less that an illness like Ebola will infect large numbers of Americans. Our country, like most developed countries, appears to have the tools needed to contain a large-scale outbreak. But if a communicable virus like Ebola one day gains a foothold inside the overcrowded cities of a developing country, it could periodically disappear and reappear in that region for years, creating health, political, and economic emergencies in many countries all at once.

The United States can lead a more ambitious multinational effort to invest in local public health systems and improve coordination when health crises occur. By mobilizing the U.S. Centers for Disease Control and Prevention more effectively, the United States can provide doctors and other health care workers, technology, medicine, beds, volunteers, logistical support, and other resources needed to help manage the risk of pandemic—and the longer-term investment needed to develop vaccines. It can also respond much more quickly and comprehensively than Washington responded to any of these previous crises.

Nothing can return us to the days before the great wars of the last century when Americans could afford not to care what happens in the rest of the world. Today there is no peacetime or wartime. We live in a world of permanent tension—a tension that must be managed. As bleak as that sounds, it's the formula that won the Cold War, restored peace and prosperity in Europe and Japan, and created the conditions that lifted hundreds of millions of people out of poverty across the developing world. America was not single-handedly responsible for those accomplishments, and our leaders made awful mistakes along the way. Make no mistake, we will make more. There are contradictions, often hypocrisy, in American foreign policy. Yet we don't live in a world that allows us to avoid every ugly moral compromise by hiding at home. Nor can we stand on more solid moral ground by insisting that we will act only for our own benefit, because the interests of America, its allies, and even its enemies are not mutually exclusive. There is no zero-sum arena in which everything bad for our enemies is good for us.

The United States emerged empowered from the world wars, but not just because we arrived late in the arena. Though compromised by our failure to honor civil rights at home, America represented an irresistible alternative to the left- and right-wing tyrannies that nearly tore the world apart. It offered opportunities for freedom and prosperity that were more widely shared than at any other place and time in history. It built national success atop a political and economic system that empowered the individual as no country has ever done. American ingenuity, imagination, and raw power have played a critical role in helping to bring about the most important global changes of the past hundred years. Isolationism and cynicism will never accomplish so much.

Americans cannot solve every problem, but this does not excuse us from the responsibility to solve the ones we can, for our own benefit and for the world. America is not, and can never be, a shining city built on a remote hilltop, a beacon of light oblivious to the darkness all around. We can't hold ourselves above and apart from others. We are citizens of a globalized world, a member of a community. We cannot simply declare independence from responsibilities that only we can fulfill.

Nor should we accept the seductive idea that foreign policy can be reduced to an easily defined set of national priorities. The Moneyballers argue that an American president can decide questions of war and peace with a simple checklist. Our leaders must always think carefully before sending soldiers into harm's way, but the so-called Powell doctrine is not as easy to apply as it might appear. Is a vital national security interest threatened? As the world becomes more deeply interconnected, a process that will only intensify over time, it becomes exponentially more difficult to clearly define those interests. A particular government may not possess a weapon capable of inflicting mass casualties within the continental United States, but it may pose real risks to energy markets, in cyberspace, via its connections with terrorist groups, or by its ability to disrupt a significant part of the global economy.

The costs and risks of modern war can never be fully analyzed in advance. Nor can we expect our president to imagine every potential consequence of American action. Is that action supported by the American people? If the men and women we have elected to lead our country believe our national security is truly at stake, it's their responsibility to build public support for the actions needed to defend us. We can't wait until the enemy starts releasing grisly videos of their atrocities to rally public backing for the actions we need to take. Do we have genuine broad international support? We should expect our leaders to try to win that backing too—but then to act in our vital interest with or without support from abroad.

Then there are the sensationalist and politicized arguments about our debt. Champions of Independent America and Moneyballers warn that until we fully relieve America's debt burden, we can't afford to lead. If we try, they warn, we will end up like some cash-strapped southern European country forced to lower its standard of living to rebalance its books. U.S. policymakers should always care about costs, because like so many other aspects of American power, the dollar's advantage over other currencies will narrow. Washington should take serious steps to reduce the national debt. But there is no Greek-style debt crisis on our horizon. The United States can pay its debts by simply printing more money. "That will trigger inflation," warn the isolationists. Take a closer look. The dollar will lose some of its advantages over time, but it will remain the world's primary reserve currency for the foreseeable future, the vital asset for central banks and commercial transactions of all kinds all over the world. That's a privilege Greece doesn't have, one that keeps international demand for dollars high and holds inflation in check.

For investors, the United States remains the safest port in any storm. That advantage keeps interest rates relatively low, despite the expansion of our national debt. Investors are not ready to bet on the longevity of the euro. China's financial system is still too underdeveloped, its economy too opaque, and its military power too much in question to support the growth of the yuan as a truly global reserve currency. Demand for dollars will remain high for many years to come, whatever the current state of the U.S. economy.

But the most important idea that separates Moneyball America from Indispensable America is a simple one: Today's globalized world of overlapping commitments, interests, and rivalries demands the kind of long-term strategic thinking that a Moneyball approach, with its focus on limited investment in limited goals for near-term results, can never produce. How many American (and global) problems are the result of short-term thinking?

Despite lessons from the financial crisis, too many senior executives at large U.S. companies still assume they're managing their company well only if investors are pushing its share price steadily higher. CEOs and company management become obsessed with maximizing quarterly profits at the expense of investment in a sound long-term growth strategy. Making matters worse, many of the largest firms' largest shareholders are managers of large portfolios who buy and sell shares quickly in search of fast profit with little interest in a company's longer-term strength and resilience.

Extend this problem to foreign policy. U.S. presidents know that the wrong sort of commitment can destroy a presidential legacy, as Vietnam did to Lyndon Johnson and as the war in Iraq will continue to tarnish opinions of George W. Bush. It's tempting for politicians to support or oppose foreign policies they believe will boost their popularity in time for the next election, and a Moneyball approach makes this problem worse by persuading them that there is little need for a broad strategic view of the world that might commit them to the wrong policy at the wrong moment. This is not the approach that won the Cold War. A policy of containing the expansion of Soviet influence guided presidents of both parties from Harry Truman to George H. W. Bush through wins and a few losses toward ultimate victory. It's an approach that requires that principles trump politics in the creation of policy.

Indispensable America

To build an Indispensable America, we must beware those who argue that military strength matters less than it used to and that we should spend much less to maintain it. The Moneyballers are right that we need an approach to foreign policy that relies on more than U.S. military might. We should use every means at our disposal—trade, investment, sanctions, cyber-capacity, espionage, energy exports, and moral suasion—to help shape tomorrow's international order. Yet nonmilitary means are not always enough to meet our challenges and by themselves are not nearly as effective as the Moneyball proponents would have us believe. Military force still matters, because the world still has its share of men with guns who are vulnerable only to superior firepower.

Sanctions can achieve limited objectives, especially when accompanied by both the credible threat of force and the promise of a reward for better behavior. But when it comes to a rogue state like North Korea, a security problem that will become more complex and dangerous over time, sanctions will have the opposite of their intended effect. These governments don't want trade and investment with the United States. They prefer an isolation that helps them manage the flow of ideas and information within their countries and gives them absolute control of wealth and power within their borders. For autocrats, exposure to the economic forces that open closed societies is always a dangerous thing.[6]

They aren't the only ones who prefer isolation. Regime loyalists with the largest stakes in their countries' relatively closed economies often prefer economic isolation, because it allows them to protect their businesses and investments from outside competition. This is true even in semi-open democracies like Ukraine, where some local oligarchs are more comfortable cutting deals with Russian crony capitalists than competing with European multinationals.

Nor is the U.S. "energy weapon" as potent as its champions like to believe. As America produces more oil and gas at home, our energy exports will boost U.S. international clout. Yet the effect can only be indirect because, unlike Saudi Arabia, Russia, and others, the U.S. government doesn't own America's natural resources, even indirectly. Though easing our dependence on foreign oil and gas is essential for national security, U.S. energy companies, owned by shareholders, will sell U.S.-produced energy to those countries willing and able to pay the highest price. And though Washington will have marginally more influence on global energy prices in years to come, it will never have the ability the Saudis have enjoyed to put irresistible pressure on prices with a politically motivated decision to increase or decrease exports.

This is not to say that our nonmilitary power should be neglected. But nonmilitary tools will always be more effective when backed with robust military power. America remains the only nation that can project that power everywhere in the world. That's an advantage that must never be underestimated. We should bolster that strength by continuing to invest in the state-of-the-art technology needed to ensure we remain not just the biggest and strongest but the smartest and most adaptable military on earth.

A Strategy for All Regions

America should use all its resources, military and nonmilitary, to make a long-term commitment to promote democracy, freedom, and open-market capitalism everywhere in the world. Yet though this strategy is crucial to America's (and the world's) future, it will take decades to achieve. In the meantime, just as winning the Cold War required a daily commitment to winning smaller battles and meeting smaller challenges wherever they appeared, so Indispensable America must effectively manage problems before they can be solved. Let's begin with a region-by-region approach.

There is no more important region for U.S. and global economic and security interests than East Asia. Competition among established and rising powers puts the world's most economically dynamic neighborhood at risk, and only the United States can keep the peace. The central challenge will be both to engage China and to limit the threats it poses for its neighbors. To do this, Washington must create a mutually profitable investment agreement with Beijing while deepening trade and security ties with Japan, China, South Korea, Indonesia, and the Philippines. These are the countries that will prove most important in decades to come for Asia's peace and its lasting economic strength. Finalizing both the Trans-Pacific Partnership and bilateral investment treaties with both China and India will be central to this plan.

There are two more things Washington must accomplish if it

is to reach its longer-term foreign policy goal in East Asia. It must work with China's government in every area of common interest, but it must also take actions that enrich, empower, and embolden China's people to bring about change inside their country. For China's government, Washington must pledge to help manage the fallout created by the eventual implosion of North Korea. It's in America's interest for the United States to lead the effort not only to lock down the DPRK's nuclear stockpile, but also to ensure that the more than twenty million North Koreans suddenly set adrift by their government's collapse don't blow an economic hole in the heart of the region and create an enormous humanitarian crisis, a burden that will otherwise fall mainly on China to manage. A cooperative behind-the-scenes effort to coordinate plans for the eventual reunification of Korea can help build trust between Washington and Beijing while treating a long-standing security headache that keeps leaders in both capitals constantly on edge.

The Moneyballers are right that the United States should also share technology with Chinese firms that helps the two countries cooperate on plans to use energy more efficiently and with less damage to the environment. The Chinese leadership has already declared energy efficiency and cleaner air and water a national priority. A comprehensive international agreement to sharply reduce carbon emissions to combat global warming may well be beyond reach. But America and China will be the world's two biggest carbon emitters for the foreseeable future, and a joint effort to develop game-changing technologies that reduce energy dependence and pollution in both countries will serve their national interests.[7]

Most important, Washington must reinforce the process of mutually assured economic destruction by drawing China into an ever-tighter web of economic interdependence through increasing levels of trade and investment. This too will reinforce trust while raising the cost for China of any action that destabilizes the United States, its economy, or its overseas interests. Washington must call on China's leaders, and the governments of every other authoritarian state, to respect the human rights of their citizens. That's a bedrock principle in international relations. But U.S. behavior will be much less threatening for China's leaders if it also strengthens China's economy. If Washington can accomplish all this, China's leaders will worry less about U.S. calls for freedom of speech, more access to information, and political rights for the country's citizens. This should be the core of America's long-term China strategy. Invest in a China that depends on its connection to the global economy and offer consistent long-term support for the enrichment, empowerment, and freedom of the Chinese people.

In the Middle East, the Moneyballers might lead you to believe that the surge in U.S. domestic energy production means Washington can worry less about the future of the region. Keep a few bases in the area and let its various conflicts burn themselves out. It's not that simple, because hydrocarbons will remain a central part of the world's energy mix for years to come. This is the region where universal democratization will face its greatest challenge. From Algeria to Egypt and Libya to Iraq, these are the countries that remind us that elections alone can never create democracy.*

In the near term, the rivalry pitting Saudi Arabia against Iran is the focal point of virtually all security worries, because their (often violent) competition plays out in one form or another in almost every important country in the region. If Washington begins to behave as if the security of Israel and tanker traffic through the Persian Gulf are all America cares about, the Saudi-Iranian confrontation will eventually put the stability of the entire Middle East

---

* Political scientist Samuel Huntington argued that a country becomes a democracy after it has held two elections in which the incumbent party is voted out of office.

at risk. Improving relations and rebuilding a minimum of trust with both will help Washington avoid that nightmare.

What are the greatest obstacles to democracy and freedom in the Middle East? First, there is the energy wealth that allows some of the region's regimes to remain financially independent of their people. Governments listen to their citizens more carefully when they depend on them for the revenue needed to maintain power. Second, in states that produce little or no energy, wealth is often concentrated in the hands of a military elite that resists political changes that might strip it of its wealth and privileges. Third, democratic elections don't always empower governments that respect democracy, and the legitimate concern that extremists remain popular with many would-be voters can be used to discredit elections by making a farce of their results. Finally, the main threats in the region, both to local governments and the United States, come from Islamic radicals willing to commit terrorist atrocities.

Long-term U.S. strategy must address each of these issues. We must continue to diversify our fuel mix away from dependence on all oil and gas, not just that produced in the Middle East. Decades from now, if America, Europe, China, India, and Japan are no longer heavily reliant on hydrocarbon energy to fuel cars, heat homes, and power industry, Middle Eastern governments that have long depended for their survival on pumping wealth out of the ground will instead have to power their economies by empowering their people. A few years ago, that might have sounded like empty election-year rhetoric. Today, technological changes in the production of both hydrocarbon and non-hydrocarbon energy make this idea much more realistic.

Next, the United States should condition military aid and trade and investment agreements to Middle Eastern governments on steps to economically empower ordinary citizens. That means investing in education that prepares them to compete in a globalized economy, and allowing women to carry that education into the workforce. It means holding all governments, friendly and unfriendly, accountable for respect for human rights. In addition, Washington can't afford to continue to sign deals that enrich only Arab oligarchs. Wealth must be widely distributed. In the beginning, Washington can set aside calls for political reform, a welcome change for autocrats still anxious over fallout from the Arab Spring and the Islamist insurrections in Syria and Iraq, in favor of an effort to empower local businesses and business owners and to boost the prospects of middle classes in all these countries.

Finally, the United States must wage relentless war on the terrorist groups that continue to plague the region from Mali and Algeria to Syria, Iraq, Yemen, and Somalia. Much of this effort must remain covert, but citizens of countries across North Africa and the Middle East will never reject autocracy when the most plausible alternative is an Islamist catastrophe.

Eurasia, the territory of the former Soviet Union, must also remain a U.S. priority, because Europe's economic vulnerability to Russia's revanchist foreign policy puts at risk the economic security of the world's largest bloc of free-market democracies. Putin's Eurasian Union is simply a reconstituted Russian Empire directed from the Kremlin that regroups as many as possible of the former Soviet states under an economic system based directly on the state- and oligarch-driven economy that has developed in post-Soviet Russia. By accomplishing this, Putin hopes to restore Russian faith in Russian power and establish a self-sustaining "managed democracy" in which the law exists to protect the state, not the rights and freedoms of the individual citizen.

The Moneyballers are right that without Ukraine, the only potential member country with a population and an economy large enough to make Putin's plan a true empire, there is no Eurasian Union worthy of the name. The events of the past two years have made it all but impossible for Russia to win the hearts and minds of a country in which 80 percent of the population is ethnic Ukrainian. Yet Russia can't allow Ukraine to follow through with plans to join Western institutions, including the European Union—and perhaps NATO—because Putin knows all too well that his own people are watching Ukraine's progress. In 1992, Ukraine's per capita income based on purchasing power parity was virtually the same as Poland's. By the end of 2014, Poland's was more than three times that of Ukraine.[8] The reason is clear: Poland joined the EU in 2004, while Ukraine has remained frozen in Russia's cold shadow. If Russia's people see Ukraine join the EU and follow in Poland's footsteps toward a more powerful economy and greater political freedom, many Russians will want the same thing.

For the near term, Washington must work with willing European partners to help Ukraine's government resist Russian pressure and enact the painful steps needed to join the European Union—and it should use sanctions and public pressure to raise the cost for Russia of every action it takes to interfere. There is no need for a U.S. military commitment. In Ukraine, Russia is a chess player struggling for a stalemate. It can use military and economic pressure to destabilize Ukraine indefinitely and make life harder for Ukraine's would-be Western partners, particularly in Europe. But it cannot persuade Ukrainians to join a Russian-led union. America need only enable Ukrainians to do what a clear majority of them already want to do. A more isolated Russia, particularly after a better-diversified global fuel mix has undermined the Kremlin's ability to rely on oil and gas exports to finance its government, can be left to undergo change on its own.

It is vitally important that the United States reinvest in its relationship with Europe, the bedrock of transatlantic stability and prosperity for the past half century. That means greater coordination on security and economic policy. It means ensuring that NATO remains the cornerstone of Western security. It means bringing the Transatlantic Trade and Investment Partnership to completion. To restore lost trust and extend counterterrorism capacity on both sides of the Atlantic, Washington should offer and invest in a joint surveillance program with NATO allies, one that focuses exclusively on potential threats to common security. The United States should work more closely with European governments to combat China's restrictions on market access and the theft of Western intellectual property. Finally, Washington must sharply improve relations with Germany, the country that will provide Europe with most of its direction in years to come.

U.S. leadership will be needed in other regions as well. In Latin America, the near-term problem is rising crime and insecurity in Central America and Mexico that will continue to create pressure on America's southern border. Over the longer term, Washington has an opportunity to improve relations with Latin America's most important rising power: Brazil. Tighter U.S.-Brazilian ties can build a hemisphere-wide consensus in favor of both democracy and sustainable free-market capitalism to help the citizens of countries like Argentina, Venezuela, and Ecuador build political and economic models that look more like those in Brazil, Mexico, and Chile.

In Africa, Washington must do much more to deepen commercial ties that expand U.S. access to some of the world's fastest-growing economies and middle classes. Stronger security relations with governments in North and East Africa can ensure long-term continuity in Washington's ability to combat terrorist groups like al-Shabaab in Somalia and Kenya, al-Qaeda in the Islamic Maghreb in Mali, al-Qaeda in the Arabian Peninsula in Yemen, and the Islamic State in Syria and Iraq. The United States can't wait until these groups hit a U.S. target before working hard to disrupt and dismantle their operations.

There must be a more coherent strategy even for the Arctic. As Arctic ice melts, competition for access to new energy and other natural resources will increase. To profit from opportunities to share in energy exploration and production in the region, Washington must strengthen the governance of Arctic offshore oil and gas development. It must also lead a coordinated effort of the eight Arctic states to protect freedom of the seas—and to ensure that the sharply increased shipping traffic this freedom will allow doesn't inflict more unnecessary damage to the region's air and water.

Think Big

Beyond the region-by-region approach, the United States is indispensable because it is the only country with the power and resources to both underwrite global security and support a general prosperity. First, there is the support that Americans can provide for the world's poorest people. Some argue that too many of our tax dollars are used to fight poverty in other countries. Beyond the moral argument that we should do what we can to help others who need help, let's remember that another nation's poverty can threaten Americans by creating a perfect breeding ground for wars that destabilize our allies and trade partners, and for terrorism, crime, and infectious disease.

In addition, aid directed toward fighting poverty is a much smaller part of federal spending than many Americans realize. Just 0.7 percent of the U.S. federal budget was spent for that purpose in fiscal year 2014. That's a total of $23.4 billion. Sound like a lot?

According to Oxfam, an NGO, in 2014 the average American tax-payer spent about $80 on development assistance to foreign countries. He also spent $101 on candy, $126 on lawn care, and $204 on soft drinks.[9] Even a cynic can see that $80 a year is a small price to pay to help alleviate suffering and safeguard our security.

The United States should also reinvest in the strength and resilience of Western institutions that have done much and can do much more to promote democracy and economic development. It should continue to help stabilize the global economy through its funding of and influence within the International Monetary Fund (IMF), an institution made up of 188 member states created to "foster global monetary cooperation, secure financial stability, facilitate international trade, promote high employment and sustainable economic growth, and reduce poverty around the world."[10] The IMF does this by monitoring economies, lending to those that need emergency help, and providing technical assistance to governments that need it.[11] Washington wields extraordinary influence within the IMF, not just by virtue of its voting share within the organization, but because the IMF could not continue without U.S. financial and political support.

Since the United States created the IMF and other international institutions in the aftermath of World War II, Washington has used the promise of IMF funding to promote democratic and market reforms intended to make recipient countries and their economies stronger and more resilient. What right, asks the Independent America supporter, does Washington have to use the IMF to pressure other governments for change? None at all—until those governments apply for IMF funding. No government is entitled to a bailout, and international lenders have every right to insist that the money they lend be used according to the terms of the agreement they negotiate with the recipient. Today, governments around the world can draw on funding from many other sources, but the IMF remains an extraordinarily valuable tool for investing and building more stable economies. The United States should make similar long-term investments in the World Bank and World Trade Organization.

Finally, there is trade. No, trade does not always create widely shared benefits. A trade agreement can enrich all who sign it, but the devil remains in the details. The reality that trade doesn't benefit everyone equally, however, is not a good reason for Americans to turn their backs on new opportunities. The United States can support a general prosperity by leading an effort to expand international trade ties. The Trans-Pacific Partnership, the Transatlantic Trade and Investment Partnership, and bilateral investment treaties with China and India offer extraordinary opportunities to prove the power of trade, investment, and free-market capitalism to lift billions of people out of poverty and into a truly global middle class.

Values

If there is one defining difference between the Moneyball and Indispensable approaches to U.S. foreign policy, it's in the power of values to remake the world. Our values are central to our longer-term effort to promote security through freedom.

At 5,525 miles, the U.S.-Canada border is the world's longest undefended international boundary. It's not a secret that the United States is militarily stronger than Canada, but the values that the two countries share give both sides confidence that Washington is unlikely to launch a surprise invasion. The next time you're reading the latest news story about a conflict somewhere in the world apparently driven by "ancient hatreds"—between Sunni and Shia or Israelis and Palestinians or Serbs and Muslims—remember that though Germany and France fought three wars between 1870 and 1945, it's difficult now to imagine the forces that could sever the ties that bind those two countries. Those ties are based on the political, economic, and ideological values they share.

The greatest shortcoming of the Moneyball approach to foreign policy is that it underestimates the power of values to shape the international system. In a world without them, only an always un-stable balance of power could prevent war among the major pow-ers. Yet despite the violence that continues to stoke conflict in some parts of the developing world, war among the world's wealthiest states has become all but unthinkable. Not all of those countries are democracies, but each draws its political durability from its ability to profit from the current international system.

The institutionalization of shared values began in the immedi-ate aftermath of World War II. In fact, the Marshall Plan is not a Moneyball idea. It's true, of course, that Americans didn't send bil-lions of dollars to help Europe rebuild as a gesture of goodwill; Washington was making a shrewd investment in Western Europe's ability to halt the westward spread of communism. It was a care-fully calculated plan to invest a large sum now to avoid the need to sacrifice a monumental sum—and tens of thousands of American lives—later. But it was successful because its architects understood that shared faith in democracy and capitalism would ensure that Marshall Plan funds would be money well spent. Shared values were central to the success of the Marshall Plan and to Cold War victory. Only the United States can be the world's indispensable nation, because only America has the means and the will to broaden and deepen the web of shared values that can stabilize international politics and the global economy, bolstering America's long-term se-curity and prosperity.

To promote American values is not to push blindly for "people power" revolutions around the world. It's foolish and dangerous to believe that every country is ready to hold national elections. Democratization begins by creating a public expectation that political leaders have a responsibility to those they govern, one that extends beyond providing for their immediate needs toward the creation of longer-term political and economic opportunities. It requires the construction and protection of governing institutions designed to protect the rights of the individual, not just the stability of the state. It depends on public access to reliable information. It demands transparency and accountability from those with power. It is a day-to-day, inch-by-inch struggle to advance a set of political and economic principles. It is a long-term bet, and, like the Marshall Plan, it's an investment that must be made with no guarantee of success.

Beyond the influence that America tries to extend within individual countries, American power—political, economic, and military—should be used to ensure that no country denies the right of its neighbors to embrace these values. In short, each country must respect the freedoms of others. That's why those who protest the expansion of NATO into former communist countries like Poland, Hungary, and the Czech Republic, or even into former Soviet states Lithuania, Latvia, and Estonia, are guilty of shortsighted, cynical Moneyball thinking. For those countries, the history of the twentieth century was a story of domination by outside powers. It is morally wrong to allow Russia a veto over choices made by the democratically elected governments of those countries. More to the point, we should recognize that Russia's objection to this expansion is based not on fears of a NATO invasion of Russia but on the Kremlin's fear, as noted earlier, that Russian citizens will notice when membership in Western institutions and an embrace of Western values help former communist countries become stronger and wealthier.

The promotion of our values abroad also makes us stronger at home by drawing immigrants to our country to make America better. Americans believe in self-determination. Attracting others who share our values powers our democracy and our economy. What does China stand for? What does Russia represent? America, for all its many shortcomings, is the embodiment of the principle that national strength grows from personal freedom. We must invest in that ideal both at home and abroad.

Democracy and Freedom

The most important of our principles are democracy and the freedom of the individual. Democracy is not simply a system of government in which leaders are chosen by competitive elections. It's also a system in which freedoms of speech and assembly are accepted and protected, a free press holds government accountable, institutions of government derive their power from citizens rather than political elites, and the civil and human rights of all citizens are protected.

The argument for democracy promotion is not just a moral one. There is no denying that America's power advantages have narrowed in recent years, and it has become more difficult for Washington to use military might, economic power, and diplomatic clout to get what it wants. America needs allies. The United States should invest in and promote democracy abroad because democracies are likely to prove better partners. There are many reasons why.

First, democracies are more predictable. Their governments better reflect the views of their people, making them less prone to abrupt changes in worldview and policy direction than a government brought about by dynastic succession, military coup, or revolution. Democracies share a common set of fundamental values, making it easier to build a lasting consensus among them.[12] They tend not to go to war with one another,[13] they don't support terrorism, and they are much less likely to produce man-made humanitarian disasters.

They also tend to value peace and stability, because they are more likely to build market economies and become wealthier, making them better trade partners and giving them more to lose from armed conflict. Democracies rely on rule of law, which guarantees the sanctity of contracts and respect for private property, a fundamental building block for lasting (and broadly shared) economic success. In fact, of countries with populations of at least six million people, the fifteen wealthiest nations in the world, measured by per capita income, are all democracies.[14] Much has been made of the three-decade run of explosive growth that has lifted China's economy so far and so fast. Yet depending on how per capita income is measured, China continues to rank between eightieth and ninetieth in the world in that category. It has the world's second-largest economy (by some estimates, it's already the largest), but it is still a poor country.[15]

Some critics of democracy promotion argue that this system isn't right for every culture. Is this the right form of government for Russia or China? How much experience do either of these countries have with a system that ensures that citizens are governed with their consent? If representative democracy can thrive in South Korea, it can take hold in North Korea. If it can make inroads in Ukraine, it can grow in Russia. If it can flourish in Taiwan, it can succeed in China. Democracy has expanded in Latin America, Africa, and parts of the former Soviet Union. Different societies hold to different cultural and political values, but democracy, institutionalized respect for human rights, and freedom of speech have become established in every region of the world—in part because of

America's successful example, and in part because American military might was used to defend these values against communist encroachment, particularly in Europe and Asia.

Over the next generation, security risks are as likely to emerge from within an individual country as from conflicts among them. Especially in weak democracies or authoritarian countries, conflicts have a way of spilling across borders, particularly in the Middle East and Africa. American investment can never by itself bring democracy to another country. But without a commitment from outsiders to promote democratic institutions, they are much less likely to take hold and put down roots.

Finally, let's not avoid the moral argument altogether. Americans, like human beings everywhere, take pride in their willingness to help those who need it. For all its flaws, democracy, more effectively than any other political system, helps individual citizens realize their natural potential by helping themselves. In other words, the ultimate reason why Americans should promote representative government is that it's the right thing to do.

How should we promote democracy? Not by invading, occupying, and staging elections in other countries. That strategy might have worked in post–World War II Japan, but as evidenced by Iraq's tortured history of the past decade, that model won't work when there is limited public support back home for the extended deployment of foreign troops needed to ensure it takes hold. There are still U.S. troops in Japan and Germany, but it would probably take another catastrophic war to build enough domestic support for that sort of long-term commitment of U.S. resources in other countries.

Instead, American policymakers should continue to use the influence and leverage provided by U.S. power and our leadership in international organizations to promote democracy over the longer term. In other words, if other governments want to build economic growth through greater access for their exports to U.S. consumers, if they want to attract American investment, if they want to enhance their security through closer ties with the U.S. military, if they want financial support from the International Monetary Fund or the World Bank, U.S. policymakers can insist that these governments make tangible investments in democratization. There will always be contradictions in U.S. foreign policy. Washington may never push as hard for democratization in Saudi Arabia as it does in Ukraine. But Washington can promote American values without ignoring the demands of U.S. interests.[16]

It's not enough to push for elections. Washington should also use all these levers to promote rule of law, freedom of speech, freedom of religion, freedom of assembly, and respect for human rights. We must support the global spread of new tools of communication to provide access to ideas and information to as many people as possible. There are those who will claim that expanding access to information is a waste of time because they haven't yet brought down some of the world's most repressive governments. But we don't need to believe that freedom of information will quickly sweep aside every autocrat to believe that expanded access to information will force governments of every stripe to respond much more often to the will of their peoples.

The Key Relationship

Finally, a few more words about the growing importance of America's relations with a country where all these values remain fundamentally compromised. The lasting importance of American ties with China extends far beyond the U.S. approach to East Asia. This will remain the world's most important bilateral relationship for decades to come. The United States needs China to succeed. We need Chinese consumers to buy our products and the Chinese government to buy our debt. We need China to help buoy the global economy. But China can only do these things if its society remains stable and its growth continues along a relatively predictable path. For the near term, that means accepting this country for what it is—an enormous developing state with an autocratic government intent on engineering unprecedented change.

But over the longer term, China's stability will depend on the willingness and ability of its leaders to adapt to changing times, to accept that society cannot forever be directed from above, and to empower China's people to determine their own destiny. In important ways, some of the men who rule China have already demonstrated considerable vision and courage by opening their economy and integrating it into the global economic system. Beijing's decision to join the World Trade Organization in 2001 and to respect its authority since then, and the wise support for this great leap forward from both Republicans and Democrats in Washington, remains a landmark achievement on the path toward a safer and more prosperous world.

By giving China a valuable stake in a rules-based international order, the United States has created a powerful set of incentives to ensure that China succeeds within the current system. Even as China pursues its national interests, even when those interests run counter to U.S. interests, even as China makes a long-term investment in its own Moneyball foreign policy, its stake in the current global order minimizes the risk of any return to the zero-sum Cold War logic that might well have ignited World War III.

Unfortunately, there is no guarantee that China will remain on this path. We can't know what will happen if things go badly wrong inside that country, if reform brings turmoil and provokes violence on a scale we have not seen. We can't know how the leadership will respond to the threat of a split within the party itself over how best to respond to the ever-increasing velocity of change. It is entirely possible that what has been gained will be lost—and that a global economy that has become increasingly dependent for its speed and direction on China's growth will drift into dark uncharted waters.

The United States should do everything possible to ensure that China's success depends on the security of the current international system. But Washington must also do what it can to empower China's people to demand greater transparency and accountability from their government and force Beijing to respect the rights of the individual. That is the crucial element of China's long-term stability. Its leaders must shift more than just wealth from the state to its citizens. They must also transfer power, slowly but surely, and in the interests of us all. Empowering China's people to demand this change should be the prime long-term objective of American foreign policy.

* * * * * * *

No, America is not in decline. We can continue to enjoy our freedom, our standard of living, and the protection of the world's mightiest military, and try hard to ignore risks and responsibilities beyond our borders. We can salute the troops on Memorial Day, thank our founders on July 4, and congratulate ourselves on all that those extraordinary Americans have done for the world.

It's not enough.

Around the world, more and more people have begun to insist that their political leaders can govern only with their consent. Many more have embraced the power of markets to build and sustain prosperity. That faith didn't appear on its own. America and its allies fought to promote and protect it. Imagine a world in which the United States had not fought for these values, a world in which Americans turned their backs on Europe and its challenges after World War II, just as they did after World War I. How might our world be different if Americans had decided not to accept the Soviet challenge?

President Eisenhower warned the world that day at the Statler Hotel that a Cold War might well be ruinously expensive. But when Moscow ignored his warning and pressed forward with plans to extend its international reach, Ike, building on a foundation laid by Harry Truman, committed America to what he knew would be a long and costly confrontation. Seven U.S. presidents, Democrats and Republicans, followed their lead. When Soviet communism finally collapsed, democracy, freedom of speech, and free-market capitalism began the next phase of their long-term global advance.

Imagine the cost to the world if America decides that the job is now finished—that Americans will no longer fight for these values. As if all that can be accomplished is already done. Hundreds of millions of people have emerged from poverty over the past generation, but how many still live without hope for a better life? Hundreds of millions of people now live in countries that can legitimately be called representative democracies. Yet how many are still governed without their consent?

America can't liberate all these people from poverty or autocracy with its military alone, and it will take time to promote lasting positive change. But there is much that Americans and our allies can and must do to lead others toward the values that history shows can be sustained for the good of all.

Let's return to the quiz. Here is how a champion of Indispensable America might answer (in italics with a brief explanation for that choice).

An Indispensable America Answer Key

1. Freedom is:

    a. *The right of every human being.*

    b. Fragile. Americans must protect it right here at home.

    c. In the eye of the beholder.

Americans didn't invent the hunger for freedom. It's a universal value. But America is uniquely capable of helping people around the world win basic freedoms from those who would deny them.

2. America is:

    a. Exceptional because of what it represents.

    b. *Exceptional because of all it has done for the world.*

    c. Not an exceptional nation. America is the most powerful, but that doesn't mean it's always right.

No nation in history has done more to ensure that leaders in other countries must answer to their citizens. This work is not finished.

3. Which of these statements best expresses your opinion?

    a. America will be better off if we mind our own business and let other countries get along the best they can.

    b. *America must lead.*

c. The primary purpose of U.S. foreign policy should be to make America safer and more prosperous.

Only America can promote and protect basic freedoms on a global scale.

4. China is:

a. America's greatest challenge and greatest opportunity.

b. The place where too many American jobs have gone.

c. *The world's largest dictatorship.*

China will never be secure and prosperous until it unleashes the true potential of its people. In today's interconnected world, America cannot be secure and prosperous in a world in which China is unstable and poor.

5. America's biggest problem in the Middle East is that:

a. *Washington supports the region's dictators rather than its people.*

b. Washington ignores small problems until they turn into big ones.

c. Washington believes it can manage an unmanageable region.

America's leaders too often treat the Middle East's symptoms rather than its disease—the unwillingness of governments to allow citizens to realize their human potential.

6. U.S. spy capabilities:

a. Will always be a double-edged sword.

b. Threaten our privacy.

c. *Are vital for protecting America.*

America must use every legal means to defend itself against attack.

7. The primary responsibility of the president of the United States is:

   a. To advance U.S. interests at home and abroad.

   b. To promote, protect, and defend the Constitution of the United States.

   c. *To lead.*

Without vision, there can be no lasting progress.

8. Which of the following best expresses your view?

   a. *A great leader can change the world.*

   b. A great leader must lead by example.

   c. In the real world, any leader must often choose the least bad of many bad options.

In a chaotic world, someone must lead. No nation is better equipped to lead than the United States of America.

9. Which is the most at risk?

   a. America's economy.

   b. *America's international reputation.*

    c. The respect of our leaders for America's founding principles.

The world is watching. Our allies and our enemies want to know if we intend to lead.

10. I hope that by the year 2050:

    a. America will share the burdens of leadership with reliable, like-minded allies.

    b. Americans will have created a more perfect union at home.

    c. *American leadership will have helped as many people as possible around the world topple the tyrants who deny them the freedom they deserve.*

America cannot remain prosperous and secure in an unstable world.

CHAPTER 6

Question Mark America

Too many Americans are worried about the future facing our children. Meanwhile, competition within the global economy has grown more fierce. So we can't simply afford to ignore the price of these wars.

—Barack Obama, West Point, New York, December 1, 2009

There are those who oppose identifying a time frame for our transition to Afghan responsibility. Indeed, some . . . would commit us to a nation-building project of up to a decade. I reject this course because it sets goals that are beyond what can be achieved at a reasonable cost, and what we need to achieve to secure our interests.

—Barack Obama, West Point, New York, December 1, 2009

Our cause is just, our resolve unwavering. We will go forward with the confidence that right makes might, and with the commitment to forge an America that is safer, a world that is more secure, and a future that represents not the deepest of fears but the highest of hopes.

—Barack Obama, West Point, New York, December 1, 2009

President Obama has the world thoroughly confused. In fairness to our forty-fourth president, he inherited two costly, unpopular wars, a financial crisis of historic severity, and a deeply divided nation—a complicated burden even for a president with much more foreign policy experience than Obama had. He understood in 2009 that most Americans wanted him to end those wars, avoid new ones, and avert economic catastrophe. In that respect, the president has largely delivered.

Yet no chief executive in decades has so evidently lacked a clear foreign policy focus. In his speeches on America's role in the world, his rhetoric has sometimes been as grandiose as anything Ronald Reagan, Bill Clinton, or George W. Bush ever said on America's greatness and responsibility to lead. Does Obama genuinely believe that America "will always be the one indispensable nation in world affairs"?[1] He has said so, but a look solely at his first-term pivot to Asia, the shift of resources from other parts of the world to ensure an active engagement of authoritarian China while courting its neighbors to hedge against China's expansion, suggests a sometimes shrewd, always cautious practitioner of Moneyball. Is Obama willing to set aside American values whenever and wherever they conflict with U.S. interests? At still other times, he has gone further than any president since the start of World War II to insist that America's limited means must set the scale of its foreign policy aspirations. That's the message he sends when he warns that "we can't simply afford to ignore the price of these wars" and promises to "spend every minute of every day doing everything in my power to make this economy work."[2]

In reality, America no longer has a foreign policy strategy. The president says we must mind the costs, even as he tells foreign leaders what they must and must not do. As if foreign leaders haven't noticed that Obama lacks public support for costly action. As if threats of "serious consequences" are enough to persuade them to do what we want. His Republican critics speak as if all we must do is "lead," without explaining what that means and what it would cost. Arm our allies. Bomb the bad guys. Wave the big stick. Show them you mean business. We'll hear more of these hollow calls to arms as the next class of presidential candidates strides onstage. That should worry us, because the disconnect between what we say and what we do mattered less when American power spoke for itself. Those days are gone, at least for now. We must choose a strategy, and our words must align with it.

It's easy for politicians to avoid tough foreign policy choices when our mistakes seem to have little impact on our country and its future. But the world will continue to become a much less predictable and more dangerous place in coming years, and if the next president bounces from one challenge to the next without a larger vision of America's role in the world, and if our words continue to run far ahead of our actions, we will soon face more foreign policy problems and crises than any president could hope to manage.

Refuse to Choose?

Before I detail why that is, let's take a serious look at an alternative view. Maybe it's wiser to create a kind of "no-strategy strategy," one designed to keep adversaries guessing without committing America to fights we don't want. If Washington makes clear exactly where Americans will and will not intervene, we're encouraging others to grab every piece of land we say we won't fight for. We're inviting them to attack every principle we aren't prepared to defend and create maximum trouble on the safe side of every red line we draw. Worse still, if we encourage adversaries to walk right up to that line, momentum can send them stumbling across it, forcing us to respond when we might not want to. So that argument goes.

Isn't it smarter to let others guess where we will and will not fight? Creation of a detailed foreign policy doctrine can push the U.S. government into commitments the American people might not support. Why commit ourselves to red lines we might later have to abandon? Look to history. We lurched our way into an unnecessary war in Vietnam by accepting the "domino theory," the Cold War–era conviction that unwillingness to confront communists anywhere would encourage them to advance everywhere. That assumption led us to mistake Vietnam's civil war for a broader communist challenge. A less doctrinaire approach would have saved tens of thousands of American lives. In addition, a strategy of creative ambiguity has helped to defend Taiwan's independence and to minimize the risk of war with China. America is not committed to defend Taiwan under all circumstances, but China can't prepare an invasion without worrying that its actions might provoke a conflict with the United States. Keep your enemies guessing so that even when you do less, they aren't sure where they can afford to test your resolve.

Maybe it's not a bad thing to keep even our allies guessing. Since the end of World War II, Americans have assumed responsibility for the security of Japan and Germany. Those countries have grown rich in part because U.S. protection allows them to spend relatively little on their own defense. Seventy years later, American taxpayers might well wonder why they're still paying to protect two of the world's wealthiest countries. Yet Germany and Japan's security dependence on Washington offers benefits, and we don't want to lose most of our influence with their governments. By keeping our intentions ambiguous, maybe we can preserve our clout with Tokyo and Berlin even as they hedge their bets on our future intentions by spending more on their own defense. For Washington, that's the best of both worlds.

Perhaps improvisation has worked for Obama. The expertly orchestrated action that took down Libya's Muammar Qaddafi saved thousands of Libyan lives in places Qaddafi promised to destroy. Obama's decisions not to launch a similar assault on Syria's Bashar al-Assad or offer U.S. or NATO military support for Ukraine were wise, because they were much less likely to be successful and would have left Americans responsible for the inadvertent killing of thousands of civilians. None of these conflicts directly threatened U.S. national security. All three tested our commitment to prevent humanitarian crises. But wasn't Obama wise to approach these similar problems with different strategies? Some might argue that Washington should be consistent in its approach to China's conflicts with its neighbors. But shouldn't the president draw a much harder line against Chinese aggression in the East China Sea than in the South China Sea? After all, China's adversary in the East China Sea, Japan, is a U.S. ally. China's main antagonist in the South China Sea, Vietnam, is not.

In today's fast-changing world, isn't flexibility a crucial advantage? Priorities change. We want to build American power from within, but we must also keep the ability to respond quickly and forcefully to various forms of crisis. And we can't afford in the name of philosophical consistency to make costly, dangerous promises we might not be able to keep. Why tell the world in advance what we consider important and what we will and will not do?

Too Much Risk

Here's why that approach won't work. As I argued in chapter 1, Washington now has less ability to get what it wants from other governments than at any time since the end of the Cold War. That's not a well-kept secret. Everyone knows that the American people want their leaders to do less. The president and U.S. lawmakers should accept that the world has changed, and that America's international influence is in decline, even if the country itself is not. If they ignore this reality, friendly governments will conclude that they can no longer trust U.S. policymakers or their judgment. Unfriendly governments will assume that Washington overestimates its ability to carry out its own threats. Washington can't bluff. It isn't holding a strong enough hand.

Nor can we afford to make up our foreign policy as we go along. Following a trip to Asia in April 2014, President Obama used an off-the-record briefing with reporters to offer a simple definition of his foreign policy doctrine. "Don't do stupid stuff,"* he reportedly said, an awkward attempt at an earthier rendition of "First, do no harm."[3] Assuming the president meant for the world to take this comment at face value, he offered a glimpse of his strategic thinking that is both purely improvisational and defined entirely by things he won't do. A few weeks later, Hillary Clinton, Obama's first-term secretary of state, made news with pointed criticism of her former boss's words. "Great nations need organizing principles, and 'Don't do stupid stuff' is not an organizing principle," she told journalist Jeffrey Goldberg.[4]

In October 2014, Susan Rice, Obama's national security adviser, invited a group of foreign policy experts to visit the White House

---

* The president reportedly used a stronger word than "stuff." This is the rendition of his quote that didn't violate the editorial guidelines of most media outlets that reported it.

and to offer their feedback on administration policy. Among the criticisms the guests offered, according to the *New York Times,* was a White House delay in releasing its "national security strategy," a document mandated by Congress that details the administration's foreign policy goals. According to unnamed sources present at the meeting, Rice dismissed this complaint. "If we had put it out in February or April or July," she said, "it would have been overtaken by events two weeks later, in any one of those months."[5]

In other words, "We can't set down a foreign policy strategy with a shelf life longer than thirty days because the world is changing too quickly."

We do need organizing principles to help us develop a coherent approach to the world and to define our role in it. Sticking to these principles helps a foreign policy team establish credibility, a vital asset. If Washington wants to lead, it must call on allies to take risks, but security guarantees are useless unless it's clear the United States will honor them. Sanctions won't work unless other countries make sacrifices to respect and enforce them, and they won't make those sacrifices if they don't believe Washington means what it says. Governments will not ask local industries to reduce carbon emissions to protect the environment unless they believe that Americans will honor their pledge to do the same. And when the president draws a red line, an adversary crosses that line, and Washington does nothing, the failure to act calls into question every commitment that president has made in the past and will make in the future. It's cheaper and safer to draw a red line than to use force, but only when the threat is credible.

An ambiguous, improvised foreign policy invites rivals and enemies to test U.S. intentions. Allies don't know how much responsibility to accept for their own security. Some will take risks, expecting support that isn't coming. Others will try to adapt to a world without

U.S. leadership. But because Washington refuses to make clear which commitments it will honor and which it won't, these governments won't have the domestic support they need to spend the money and accept the risks to take more responsibility for their own security. Our more self-confident allies might want to play a larger leadership role on challenges that are important to them, but they're much less likely to step forward if they aren't sure we have their backs. Mixed signals from the president and senior members of Congress might serve their political interests, but they're terrible for policy, because they ensure that the risk of miscalculation, on all sides, will grow. Creative ambiguity can also allow U.S. policymakers to avoid tough choices altogether, ensuring that even Americans don't know where the United States will push back and where it won't.

Our allies deserve better. The United States has never accomplished anything important on its own. Every accomplishment we celebrate was achieved with vital support from our friends and partners. Those who have stood with us over the years need to know whether they can call us when they need us and expect America's president to pick up the phone. Our allies and adversaries must know whether the United States intends to lead, whether it will fight only for its core interests, or whether others must adapt to a world in which the Americans aren't coming.

There is one more interested party who deserves to know what our government intends: the American voter. As the next election campaign floods the airwaves with grand campaign promises, let's remember that the foreign policy decisions our leaders make will have enormous implications for life at home, for the strength and resilience of our economy, for the men and women of our military, and for the future of the United States itself. The voter deserves to know what the candidates believe and how they would make those decisions. Americans need to know what they're voting for.

Eurasian and European Choices

Here are some real-world examples that make clear why America must choose and communicate its choices to friends and foes alike. Start with Eurasia, the territory of the former Soviet Union and its immediate surroundings. Russia is losing strength. As it becomes weaker in coming years, as Vladimir Putin's standing at home becomes less sure, Russian foreign policy will become even more unpredictable than it is now. The need to prepare for an increasingly erratic Kremlin demands that Europeans understand what they can and cannot expect from Washington. Only then can Europe prepare to manage these threats, alone or with Washington's help.

Why is Russia weakening? Its government continues to depend for revenue and growth on energy exports. Far from diversifying its economy over the past decade, Russia has become more reliant on pumping wealth from the ground rather than on the ingenuity and innovative potential of its people. This dependence leaves it exposed like no other economy of its size to fluctuations in oil prices. Demand for oil has probably peaked in the developed world as industrialized economies further diversify the mix of fuels they use to power their economies. Russia can turn toward emerging China to buy more of its energy, as it did in 2014 when Putin and Chinese president Xi Jinping signed a thirty-year $400 billion contract for Russian natural gas exports to China.[6] But with less Western demand for Russia's product, China and others will drive a harder bargain on price, leaving Russia's treasury with less revenue. The U.S. energy revolution, detailed earlier in the book, will promote the use of new technologies that help other countries find and produce more of their own hydrocarbon energy, increasing global supply and putting further downward pressure on prices.

Russia is unlikely to reduce its dependence on oil and gas exports as long as Putin holds power, because he uses them as tools (sometimes weapons) of his foreign policy. Yet many of the country's existing energy fields are past their prime, and Russia needs Western-made advanced technologies to access tight oil and offshore Arctic deposits to continue to increase production. U.S. and European sanctions, imposed in response to the conflict in Ukraine, will limit Russia's ability to buy them, and Russia won't be able to maintain, much less increase, future production levels. It's a recipe for slow and steady decline—of energy production and of Russia's economy. For the moment, Russia holds cash reserves worth hundreds of billions of dollars, a substantial rainy-day fund. But it will rain on Russia more often in years to come as lower revenue from oil exports reduces spending on pensions and social services and reduced support for unprofitable industries increases unemployment.

Yet Russia's decline is not good news for the United States, for Europe, or for Russia's neighbors. As its economy slows, public frustration with government will extend beyond Moscow and St. Petersburg into the Russian heartland. President Putin's political standing will become more precarious, encouraging him to try to regain lost public support by again flexing Russia's muscles in its old Soviet neighborhood. That will intensify Moscow's conflict with the West, not just over Ukraine, but over states like Latvia, Estonia, and even Poland—countries that are treaty allies of the United States.

Here is the danger of Question Mark America. If U.S. (and European) sanctions make disruptive Russian behavior more likely, is Washington committed to managing this long-term threat? The Obama administration's awkward combination of tough talk and limited sanctions leaves plenty of doubt on what Washington will and won't do. If the United States decides to try to reengage Russia, to give Moscow incentives for cooperation with the West, that's the message the president must sell. The current strategy, one that says,

"Do what we ask or we'll punish you gradually and at the margins," will not work.

If America's next president decides that a policy of constructive reengagement with Russia is doomed to fail, Putin and his successors must know where Russia will meet immovable resistance. Will the United States honor its commitment to treat an attack on a NATO ally as an attack on America itself? If Russian troops one day cross the border into Latvia, whatever the pretext, will the president of the United States declare war on Russia? President Obama has *suggested* that he would, but he hasn't said it.[7] Europe needs to know. America's men and women in uniform, their families, and American taxpayers need to know. Leave it ambiguous and Moscow might one day decide to find out what it can get away with. Encourage ethnic Russians inside the country to start trouble. Complain about how the Latvian government treats them. Pledge to defend them and see how Washington reacts. If it doesn't react forcefully, move weapons across the border into the country. If that doesn't draw a sharp reaction, send in some troops.

Russian aggression in Ukraine does not automatically demand that America take military action. A Russian invasion of Latvia, Estonia, or any other NATO member is a different matter. If Washington confirms its NATO commitment to Latvia's security, it must honor that commitment. If it doesn't, if the United States will not defend Article 5 of the North Atlantic Treaty, then NATO has forfeited all credibility. Public support for the organization within member states will evaporate. Russia will no longer take the alliance seriously. If U.S. policymakers determine now that it is not in America's interest to keep its promise to Latvia, Washington should call on European governments to build the domestic public support needed to invest in a capable collective European defense that does not include U.S. forces.

Questions about Russia also bear directly on the future of U.S. relations with Europe. Is it in America's long-term interest to remain as final guarantor of Europe's security? As I detailed in chapter 1, there is already a growing divide in transatlantic relations. Washington and its European allies comprise the most powerful potential coalition of capable and like-minded allies in history. Together, they built the foundation of the post–World War II global order. But though the two sides must worry about Vladimir Putin and what he might do next, that concern is much stronger in Europe, which is much more at risk and has much more to lose from Russian military aggression and economic retaliation. In this case, shared political values may not be enough to counter the impact of increasingly divergent interests. The worst outcome, for America and for Europe, is for America's next president to say one thing and do another or to refuse to decide what America will and won't do until Washington is put to the test.

Russia is not the only source of U.S.-European division. American and European leaders will also find themselves at odds as access to Chinese consumers pushes U.S. and European companies into an increasingly high-stakes competition with one another. Transatlantic commercial relations are suffering in other areas as well. In 2014, U.S. federal prosecutors accused French bank BNP Paribas of helping clients evade U.S. sanctions on Iran and Sudan. The bank pleaded guilty to criminal charges and paid $8.9 billion in fines. The United States has targeted other European banks, including Credit Suisse, UBS, and Barclays on tax evasion, interest-rate fixing, and other charges.[8] Add European allegations of American espionage, and things are going from bad to worse. It's not that the United States should pass on prosecuting foreign banks that violate U.S. law. It's that a transatlantic relationship that often depends more on commercial than on security ties requires deeper

cooperation in other areas on which to build a long-term commitment to the alliance. Higher-priority work toward the Transatlantic
Trade and Investment Partnership would help. If Washington
sends mixed signals on these issues, Europe will create its own Russia policy and its own China policy, and will adopt a more confrontational approach to commercial disputes with the United States.

Middle East Choices

Over the next generation, a strengthening Iran, a weakening Saudi
Arabia, their intensifying rivalry, and the expectations their governments have for U.S. foreign policy will determine how much turmoil we can expect from the Middle East. As Iran's mullahs work
to build their credibility with a new generation of Iranian young
people and as Saudi Arabia edges toward a new generation of royal
leadership, the Iranian-Saudi competition for regional dominance
will play out in countries across the region. We will see this conflict
in Iraq, where a Shia-led government in Baghdad and well-funded
Sunni ISIS militants will continue their life-and-death long-term
struggle for control of that country and its oil. We'll see it in Syria,
where an Iran-backed government will have to fend off more challenges from ISIS and other Saudi-backed rebel groups. We'll see it
in Lebanon, where Iran's proxy Hezbollah will continue to shape
the country's politics. We'll see it in Bahrain, where a Saudi-backed
Sunni monarch will scan the horizon every morning for new
threats from the country's Shia majority. We'll see it Yemen, a
country made almost impossible to govern by the competing demands of warring political and tribal factions.

The region's second emerging trend will be the further radicalization of Islamist politics. This problem is hardly new. A genera-

tion ago, the ruling party of Algeria, the National Liberation Front (FLN), succumbed to internal and external pressure for political change and allowed a rewrite of the country's constitution that permitted multiparty elections. In December 1991, after a religious party known as the Islamic Salvation Front (FIS) swept a first round of parliamentary elections, the ruling party canceled the second round and brought democratization to an abrupt halt. These events radicalized the Islamic opposition and triggered a decade-long civil war in Algeria that killed tens of thousands of people. The bloodshed proved a harbinger of trouble to come elsewhere in the region.

With the arrival of the Arab Spring in 2011, hope grew that new elections might deliver Egypt (and other Arab states) from an era of dictatorship and poverty into a brighter and more open future. Instead, the Muslim Brotherhood won the election, and President Mohamed Morsi tried to grant himself almost unlimited political power and to introduce a new constitution that observed principles of religious law. In response, Egypt's military removed him from power, threw him in jail, and established a new army-led dictatorship. Crucial financial support for Egypt's new military government flowed in from Gulf monarchies fearful of the long-term threat that religious parties posed to the region. As in Algeria, once opened, the lid on Pandora's box was hastily slammed shut.

The Egyptian coup strengthened the arguments of religious radicals that power and liberation must be won through bloodshed, not the ballot box. Though isolated militant attacks will continue, Egypt's military government has established firm control of the country's territory. Iraq's government has no such dominance. In 2014, Islamist militants, armed with training and experience gained in Syria's civil war and financing from sympathetic Sunni groups in Saudi Arabia and elsewhere, crossed the poorly defended border into Iraq, where an Iran-backed, Shia-led government in Baghdad had excluded most Sunnis from the political process. ISIS seized cities across northern Iraq in 2014 and became the best-funded terrorist organization in history. Here, the Iran-Saudi rivalry and the radicalization of Islamist politics came together to generate bloodshed and turmoil—and a conflict that will continue to develop over many years.

The terrorist threat is growing elsewhere in the region. The inability of al-Qaeda to stage a second large-scale strike on the United States or in the heart of a European city has persuaded a new generation of jihadis to focus on local targets. Beyond Syria and Iraq, we should expect terrorist challenges to continue in Egypt, Libya, Yemen, and Jordan. Militant groups from Nigeria and Mali in the west to Yemen and Somalia in the east will pose a continuous challenge. Other states will remain vulnerable. These things are easy to predict.

Other questions are not so easily answered. How will Iran use its regional influence? How will the Saudis respond to Iran's moves? How will Iran's clerics and Saudi royals respond to demand for change within their countries? Will President Recep Tayyip Erdoğan continue to polarize Turkey and undermine its influence in both the Middle East and Europe? Or will the pressure exerted by a slowing economy and public demand for great accountability force a return to the policies that helped Erdoğan and his party lift so many Turkish citizens from poverty a decade ago? Can Israelis and Palestinians empower leaders capable of finding enough common ground to finally resolve a conflict that continues to threaten Israel's existence and inflicts suffering on Palestinians? Will Libya descend into chaos? Can governments contain the threat posed by all the various forms of Islamic militancy?

The answers to these questions will be determined in part by the answer to our broader question: What role should America play in this region? Israelis need to know whether America remains a constant friend and will safeguard its security by any means necessary. Palestinians need to know whether Washington will act as an honest broker and push for political settlement. Iran's people need to know if the United States intends to engage or ignore them. After Washington's incoherent improvisational response to the Arab Spring, the Saudi and Egyptian people need to know whether America will back calls for democratization, bolster their governments in the name of stability, or leave these countries to decide their own fates. The people of Syria need to know whether Washington will enforce a ban on the use of chemical weapons. Governments in Iraq, Nigeria, Mali, Morocco, Jordan, Libya, Lebanon, Yemen, Kenya, and other countries across North Africa and the greater Middle East need to know how and whether America will help them fight terrorism within their borders. The Europeans and the Chinese need to know too, because if the United States means to stand down, it will be in both their long-term interests to step up.

Though the United States will continue to reduce its dependence on Middle Eastern oil in coming years, which costs and risks should Washington continue to accept in order to protect the flow of oil that we'll need in the meantime, the flow of oil to allies, like Japan, and to other countries crucial to the future of the global economy, like China? Though the United States needs less of the region's oil, turmoil there will continue to move energy prices, which will pose both direct and indirect threats to the U.S. economy.

If jihadis are slaughtering innocents in Iraq, Syria, Nigeria, or Somalia, does America have a moral responsibility to intervene? Do Americans have a duty to defend democracy in this region? Where do our interests and responsibilities begin and end? Americans need to know. Don't let those who would lead us evade these questions. Once we have elected them, they will have to choose, and it's our future that their choices will determine.

East Asian Choices

The toughest choices will be for U.S. policy toward East Asia, because it is here that opportunities for America are greatest and risks are highest. The future of China will remain the region's most important question mark for years to come. Its leadership will try to enact reforms that help China make the leap from a poor country with a large export-driven economy to a stable and resilient middle-class country. If the Communist Party leadership loses control of that process, if battles within the party elite over the country's future and the party's role in it spill into the open, if the economy cools too quickly, jobs are lost, and labor unrest takes on a life of its own, China will become a much more volatile place, and its leaders will try to rally public support with a more aggressive foreign policy. Given the scale of the reform challenge and the country's growing importance for global growth, the stakes for China, its neighbors, and the world economy couldn't be higher.

Japan, India, Pakistan, South Korea, Vietnam, the Philippines, Indonesia, and other Asian states will have to decide how to respond not only to China's rise and its domestic political stability but also to Washington's intentions. These countries need to know whether Americans will help them contain threats of aggression from China or leave them with responsibility for their own security. These states also want to know if Washington is prepared to offer terms they can accept to forge agreements that deepen trade and investment ties with them. The men and women asking for our votes must tell us how they would answer these crucial questions.

If the United States is to maintain a firm and open-ended commitment to the security of Japan, Washington must do it without making conflict with China inevitable. It's reasonable to ask Japan's government and its people to make the security alliance a true partnership by spending more on their own defense and by extending Japan's military reach well beyond its territorial waters. But Washington must also persuade Beijing that this shift is not meant to stunt the natural growth of China's influence, by making clear to both sides that America will not support needlessly provocative Japanese behavior toward China.

Or if Americans decide that Asia's powers must learn to live together without the U.S. military to keep them from fighting, Washington will have to make that clear for Japan, which will then need time to make the transition to an entirely new reality. If Washington expects Tokyo to take responsibility for its own security, Japanese voters must see clearly that they have no choice but to spend the money, build the defense, and rethink the future of relations with China. U.S. plans can't remain ambiguous if Japan's leaders are to persuade Japan's voters that there is no other way forward.

What's true for Japan is true for South Korea. If Americans decide that North Korea is ultimately an Asian, not an American, problem, South Korea will have to significantly adapt its defense approach. South Korea's elected leaders will have to persuade the country's taxpayers to provide much more public money to rise to the new challenge and recalculate how best to manage complex relations with both China and Japan. South Koreans also need to know what America will do when North Korea finally implodes and the costly and complicated multiyear process of Korean reunification begins. America can help by making its long-term intentions clear. If, on the other hand, the United States wants to deepen its security and commercial relations with South Korea, U.S. relations with Japan and China demand that Washington make that understood. It will minimize the risk of a North Korean military miscalculation, and it will give America greater influence over the post–North Korean Asian security landscape.

Washington must also decide how and whether to more deeply engage India. U.S. leaders have debated for years how best to improve relations with the world's most populous democracy without undermining efforts to better engage India's most powerful rivals, China and Pakistan. If Americans are to seize the opportunity provided by Indian anxiety over China's rise and Pakistan's instability to deepen political, commercial, and security ties with Delhi, the United States must make a long-term commitment to try to overcome decades of mistrust between the two countries. But if Americans conclude that it's best for the United States if India, China, and Pakistan begin to manage their territorial and sectarian disputes without U.S. involvement, the signals from Washington must be unambiguous.

The Philippines is another U.S. ally awaiting a clear signal from Washington of its future intentions. In recent years, disputes over maritime territory in the South China Sea have pushed China and the Philippines toward direct confrontation. China is already among the Philippines' largest trade partners, creating a vulnerability that the much larger China can exploit. To avoid overreliance on China and its economy, the Philippines, like Japan, has worked to improve defense cooperation with the United States and indicated an interest in joining talks on membership in the Trans-Pacific Partnership. If the Philippines is to continue hedging its bets on relations with China, the government in Manila needs to know if the United States intends to maintain its long-term presence in East Asia or whether Washington will decide that the time has come to transition toward a foreign policy focused on rebuilding American strength from within while allowing friends and foes to begin to manage their own frictions.

In addition, the election of Barack Obama seemed to signal an opportunity for much better U.S. relations with Indonesia, a dynamic multiparty democracy that is home to more than 250 million people, a country where Obama lived from ages six to ten. Hillary Clinton visited Indonesia during her first overseas trip as secretary of state in 2009. Yet U.S.-Indonesian ties have yet to live up to their potential. Indonesia, like many states in the region, would like to strengthen its political, economic, and security ties with Washington to ensure that deeper trade and investment engagement with China don't leave it overly dependent on Beijing's goodwill. If the United States wants to capitalize on this opportunity, Washington should make a clearer commitment to seize it. If Americans determine that U.S. security and prosperity are best served by a pivot from Asia toward the home front, Jakarta should know that.

Scenario Planning

Consider a few recent foreign policy mistakes and the choices that might lie ahead for a future U.S. president.

Scenario 1: In 2011, the Obama administration was caught off guard when pro-democracy demonstrators flooded the streets of Cairo to demand the ouster of President Hosni Mubarak, a stalwart thirty-year U.S. ally. How to respond? Support for democracy is a core American value. How can the United States side with an autocrat against the democratic aspirations of his people? But backing a reliable ally who has helped keep the peace in a tough neighborhood and has helped bridge the divide between Arabs and Israelis is in U.S. interests, particularly when sudden change inside Egypt might produce chaos across the country. Or maybe it was never any of our business. Following intense debate within the White House, Obama sided with the street.

A year later, the Muslim Brotherhood's Mohamed Morsi became Egypt's first democratically elected president. His attempts to grab extraordinary powers and his decision to declare martial law to quell the resulting protests persuaded Egypt's military to arrest him. The Obama administration was confronted with another choice. Should the president denounce the army's action as a coup, which would have forced Obama under U.S. law to suspend $1.3 billion in aid to Egypt? Should he side with the military? Should he make clear that Egypt's politics are not Washington's concern? Secretary of State John Kerry argued that by sidelining Egypt's elected president, the military was "restoring democracy."[9] The Obama administration sent more such mixed signals.

Now add oil to the equation. What if, a few years from now, a similar situation arises in Saudi Arabia? (Sound far-fetched? So did the fall of the Berlin Wall, the Soviet collapse, the global financial crisis, the Arab Spring, and the Eurozone crisis. Until they happened.) Public frustration triggers a cycle of protest and repression that creates dangerous levels of unrest inside the kingdom. How should America's president respond? An Independent approach might persuade the president to steer clear of this mess. Better to avoid direct involvement in a problem that Washington can't solve. It's their country. Let Saudis solve their own problems. A Moneyball strategy might guide the president to avoid taking sides until it was clear which side would win. The smart play is to refuse to stand on principles that we have no power to apply and instead to offer support for Saudi Arabia's *next* government. An Indispensable strategy might persuade the U.S. president to stand firmly on the side of democracy and rule of law, whatever the immediate consequences. If America won't stand for our values when the going gets tough, why should anyone care what we say or what we think? Worst of all, a refusal to choose would serve neither our interests nor our values.

Scenario 2: As Russia began to destabilize Ukraine in 2014, the Obama administration found itself drawn into another fight it didn't want. As it became unavoidably obvious that Russia was violating international agreements and Ukraine's sovereignty, the president made it clear that the United States would not intervene militarily but would impose sanctions on Russia that, he must have known, could not force Putin to back down. In short, Obama committed the United States to a fight he had no intention of trying to win.

Now add a much more important economic power. What if, in 2018 or 2021, China and Vietnam stumble into war and China invades Vietnam? How should the U.S. president respond? An Independent approach might lead the president to express "concern" and nothing more. Common sense suggests that China won't back down and can't be isolated. Let China and Vietnam face the consequences of their choices. If Washington is not willing to play a decisive role in this hypothetical war—and it's hard to imagine how it could play such a role—then we should make clear that their war is not our concern. A Moneyball approach might persuade the president to avoid taking sides in the conflict but to use the fear it produced in the region to build stronger military and economic ties with China's other neighbors. Don't step between China and Vietnam, but use their conflict to serve longer-term U.S. interests. An Indispensable strategy might lead the president to take a forceful stand against China's actions. No, the United States can't evict China from Vietnam, but if we won't speak forcefully against an act of naked military aggression, and find ways to impose economic and other costs on China to make clear that we mean what we say, then the president will have forfeited America's claim to stand for what's right. If there is no cost for this kind of aggression, the kind of cost that only America is willing and able to impose, we can expect a lot more aggression in the future—and not just from China. The worst choice is to do and say nothing. Those in China who favor a more muscular military approach in East Asia will have been rewarded for their boldness. The United States will lose influence across the region as China's neighbors conclude that Washington can't or won't help them. And America will have stood for nothing.

Scenario 3: In August 2012, reports surfaced that embattled Syrian president Bashar al-Assad had used, or might be preparing to use, chemical weapons against Syrian rebels. President Obama responded:

> We have been very clear to the Assad regime, but also to other players on the ground, that a red line for us is we start seeing a whole bunch of chemical weapons moving around or being utilized. That would change my calculus. That would change my equation.

Credible evidence then emerged that Assad had used the weapons, but Obama took no action—other than agreeing to a Russian-sponsored deal in which Assad promised to get rid of his chemical and biological stockpile. Three weeks later, when challenged on the "red line" comment, Obama argued that the red line he referred to was not his:

> First of all, I didn't set a red line; the world set a red line. The world set a red line when governments representing

98 percent of the world's population said the use of chemical weapons are abhorrent and passed a treaty forbidding their use even when countries are engaged in war.[10]

In the process, the president badly damaged his personal credibility—and the credibility of the United States.

Now add nuclear weapons. What if one day, at a moment of massive unrest in nuclear-armed Pakistan, the country's army deposes another elected government and imposes martial law. The turmoil in the streets is generated both by demonstrators demanding a restoration of democracy and by Islamic militants carrying out terrorist attacks in Pakistan's most densely populated cities. The new military government begins a brutal crackdown against both. The stability of the country and the security of its nuclear material are thrown into question. How does the president of the United States respond?

An Independent strategy might lead the president to recognize that the United States is merely an onlooker in this situation and that taking sides can only further poison relations with large numbers of people who will be crucial for Pakistan's future, both civilians and military officers. A Moneyball approach might persuade the president to move quickly with verbal and military support for Pakistan's new military government as it begins to take the fight to Islamic militants, our common enemy. An Indispensable approach might instruct the president to draw a clear red line: Unless the military restores the country's elected government to power, all U.S. military and economic aid for Pakistan will come to a halt. The president must then keep that promise, come what may. A military crackdown on jihadis might solve an immediate problem, but it's not the answer to the questions that have been plaguing Pakistan for decades. Rule of law, not martial law, is the long-term answer. The worst choice will be to draw a red line that we will not enforce or to offer verbal support for the civilian protesters with nothing to back it up. That would alienate both the protesters and the military, and do nothing to address the terrorist challenge that threatens them both.

Global Leadership?

There is a final fundamental question that Americans must answer. For those challenges that transcend borders—collective security, climate change, trade, the proliferation of dangerous weapons, cyber-security, and terrorism—must America lead? Is the world better off with American leadership? Is America better off? Or is it time for America to make room for others to lead? If we leave the rest of the world guessing, we will create many more problems than we solve.

To help answer these questions, consider another: Do global problems demand global solutions? This question reopens the original American debate. Are there common American problems that are best addressed in Washington, D.C.? Or is it best to allow each of the states to build its own solution? Some will argue that a local approach to problem solving makes the most sense, because it allows each state to serve as a policy laboratory where ideas can be tested—and because it allows for solutions that reflect local values. Others counter that there will always be shared challenges that cross state borders and that only a centrally agreed-upon and enforced answer can resolve these questions.

Inside the United States, this is a debate over the proper balance of decision-making authority between the governments of the fifty states and the federal government in Washington. You probably already have an opinion on whether America is best served by local or national leadership. But at the global level, it's a choice between authority at the country level and . . . what? It's difficult to imagine that many of the world's citizens want centralized global leadership. In any form. But what role should America play in helping to provide a leadership substitute? In today's world, how much can one country do to underwrite collective international security?

Should America accept this challenge? Should Washington lead coalitions of capable and like-minded partners to manage high-priority problems? Are half-measures better than nothing? Or is this responsibility dangerous and expensive enough to threaten America's future? Does climate change demand a grand international bargain? Is it foolish to believe that any such bargain is possible? Is there anything individual countries can do to address this threat on their own? Can individual nations block the proliferation of nuclear weapons, or does this issue demand a broad international response? Can an international agreement help limit the risk of terrorist attack or cyber-attack, or can these challenges only be addressed by individual governments? We can't allow our would-be leaders to ask for our votes without telling us what they believe and why they believe it.

* * * * * * *

President Theodore Roosevelt is reported to have said, "In any moment of decision, the best thing you can do is the right thing, the next best thing is the wrong thing, and the worst thing you can do is nothing."[11] I agree. That doesn't mean that the worst foreign policy mistake is to do nothing. The wars we don't fight, the deals we don't sign, the sanctions we don't impose, and the compromises we refuse to make sometimes serve us best. Instead, it means that

Americans have a choice to make, one that will define the future of our country's role in the world, and the worst thing we can do is refuse to choose. It's no good for us or for the world if we pledge to lead but fail to show up. It's dangerous for us and for the world to encourage our friends and enemies to guess at where we'll stand our ground and where we won't. Which American foreign policy is best for the world? Which is best for America?

It's time to choose.

Conclusion

All leaders lead by example whether they intend to or not.
—John Quincy Adams

I wrote this book to help you decide what you think: What sort of superpower do you believe the United States of America should be? I've presented the strongest cases I can for each of these three choices. I've argued that the worst choice of all is to refuse to choose, because I don't believe we can continue to improvise our foreign policy. We're confusing our allies, our rivals, and the American people with an incoherent approach to an increasingly dangerous world.

Indispensable?

If you've come this far, you deserve to know what I think. As I said in the introduction, I began this book unsure of how to answer my own question. I wrote it, in part, to find out. As I presented each of the three cases, I felt the emotional appeal, the strengths, and the weaknesses of each argument. Indispensable America resonates because we do live in an increasingly dangerous world, and only the United States can even attempt to lead efforts to contain the world's many conflicts. I believe that the current lack of international leadership will eventually create so much turmoil that the nations that profit most from the current system will be forced to cooperate in order to defend it. I want my country to play an important enough part in that effort to have a hand in shaping the next global order. I also believe that for all their limitations, democracy, rule of law, freedom of speech, and respect for human rights empower people around the world to realize their individual potential.

The most striking weakness of Indispensable America is that though our political leaders and office-seekers continue to adorn their speeches and talking points with poetic references to this idea, the American people continue to tell pollsters that they don't really want it. They don't want an open-ended commitment to risk American lives and spend American dollars to achieve goals of doubtful use here at home or to try to export values that others may not want. As more and more countries build the strength they need to deny our requests and resist our demands, it will become even more difficult to persuade Americans that global leadership serves our national interest—especially after the nation-building and other failed projects of the past twenty-five years.

There's also the reality that many people around the world don't consider America a leader worth following. They want less, not more, U.S. interference in their countries and their lives. They love American technology, social media, music, movies, and fashion. But like so many Americans, they don't much care what Washington thinks about how they should be governed, who their international friends should be, and how they should manage their money. How many people around the world know that America provides global public goods like conflict containment, information to help their governments fight terrorism, and a stable international financial system? How many believe that America is an arrogant, hypocritical bully that cares about nothing but its own interests? In reality, the leadership America provides hasn't changed much in recent years, but foreign perceptions of the value of that leadership have changed quite a bit since the Cold War's end.

Others will not see us as we believe we deserve to be seen. Can we blame them? Are they wrong to roll their eyes at our lectures on free and fair elections after the 2000 U.S. presidential vote was decided by court battles over "hanging chads"? Why not tune out our sermons on human rights as we offer up legalistic definitions (and redefinitions) of torture, explain away our "rendition" of foreign prisoners to countries we know will torture them, and justify the continuing operation of the prison at Guantánamo Bay? Should we expect other governments to set aside differences of opinion to support our foreign policy when we so often override their objections on issues important to them? Did the multinational effort we led in Afghanistan make our allies more secure and more prosperous? Isn't the financial crisis that continues to weigh on the global economy a result, at least in part, of the failure of U.S. lawmakers to properly regulate the country's financial system? Should our friends ignore the fact that we listen to their phone calls and read their e-mail? There may well be good answers to all these questions, but if so many citizens and political officials of other countries refuse to accept those answers, what difference does it make?

Then there are Washington's political food fights and their impact on America's international reputation. Why should the rest of the world respect our president when millions of Americans argue publicly that he is stupid or evil? In today's hyperconnected world, the sex-scandal-based impeachment of Bill Clinton, the caricature of George W. Bush as a reckless fool, and the suggestion that Barack Obama is a Muslim socialist phony tell the world that Americans no longer really care what others think of their politics—and that no U.S. president will have the reliable backing he needs to build a foreign policy with staying power.

American national shame is not a new phenomenon. The murders of John Kennedy, Robert Kennedy, and Martin Luther King Jr., battles over segregation and civil rights, the My Lai massacre in Vietnam, the surrender of Saigon, Watergate, gas shortages, hyperinflation, the Iran hostage crisis, the nuclear accident at Three Mile Island, the Iran-Contra scandal, and the invasions of Grenada and Panama all earned their share of international disdain. But that was at a time of Cold War. Given a choice between the United States and the USSR, many people around the world needed America to succeed. Not anymore. Today we present ourselves as the only option. The victor. The model. The Indispensable Nation.

The U.S. Constitution limits the power of America's commander in chief to pursue his own agenda, even if some presidents have chosen to ignore essential elements of these constraints. And for reasons that have less to do with bad decisions by Clinton, Bush, or Obama, the next president's power will be further limited by America's increasing inability to get what it wants from other governments. For all these reasons, it's hard to argue that America remains indispensable for the world's peace and security, however deeply convinced we are that our values are the best and that the world should follow our lead. That's not defeatism. That's realism. We can't lead if others won't follow.

I grew up with the Indispensable idea, and it's not an easy one to set aside. I certainly felt the pull of that argument as I wrote that chapter. Indispensable was the right strategy at the end of World War II. The United States was the only major power left standing with anything like its prewar strength. The international order was in disarray, and only America was strong enough to offer a coherent leadership vision. But we can't ignore the ways that the world has changed. America can't play the same role in 2020 that it played in 1945, 1970, or even 1990.

Moneyball?

These shortcomings make the idea of Moneyball awfully appealing. A Moneyball foreign policy would set priorities and stick to them, allowing Washington to devote its limited means to achieving our most important objectives with plans that are politically and financially sustainable. Support for a foreign policy that is designed to get more for less won't bring campaign crowds to their feet, but it represents the best American traditions of prudence and common sense. Ask our leaders to care much more about our country's bottom line. Countries aren't companies, and presidents are much more than CEOs, but in a world of unpleasant (and potentially expensive) surprises, maybe our government should look to the best American (and non-American) companies for ideas and inspiration.

How do companies become successful? How do they deliver return for their employees and shareholders? They set priorities and

make hard choices. They adapt to become stronger and more efficient. They innovate. They build flexibility into their operations to
ensure they get the best result at the lowest long-term expense.
They work hard to understand their competition and the ever-
changing environment in which they must survive and thrive. They
build partnerships based not on shared values but on the common
quest for value.

The architects of U.S. foreign policy can do the same. In particular, a Moneyball foreign policy would allow Washington to focus its attention as never before on the world's single most important
potential partnership, now and for many years to come. Fast-
changing China represents the greatest opportunity and the greatest threat to America's future, because it is well on its way to
becoming the world's largest economy, because there is a profound
economic interdependence that binds the two countries together,
and because it's not at all clear what sort of country China will be
even five years from now.

If we're wise enough to understand that democracy will come
to China only when its people will no longer accept an alternative,
we can look beyond our self-defeating attempt to remake that country's value system and build the unprecedented levels of trade and
investment that can protect and empower the citizens of both countries. If we're wise enough to develop a common approach to innovation in energy production, one based on common ingenuity and
mutual investment, the world's two largest energy consumers can
end their shared vulnerability to turmoil in the Middle East. And
if we can build genuine trust between the two governments, Washington can help contain the risk of conflict in East Asia, the world's
most economically promising region.

Building this partnership would demand hard choices about
America's relations with allies like Japan and potential allies like

India. It would require the courage to become less directly involved in the Middle East and its conflicts—including by limiting future commitments to directly defend Israel's security. This strategy would also require us to develop a finer and deeper understanding of China's internal pressures and its view of the world, and summon the courage to move beyond a moralistic approach to our foreign policy.

A crucial downside of Moneyball America: Even if a successful U.S. foreign policy depended only on Washington's wisdom and the strength of the president's will, it makes little sense to place only a few large bets in today's world of shocks and quakes. In particular, let's have the humility to admit that the success of a U.S.-Chinese partnership will depend far more on decisions made in Beijing than on those made in Washington. Though America is forever changing, our ongoing evolution carries nothing like the dramatic stakes now found in China. Can that country's current leaders survive these changes? How will they respond when they come to believe that the ruling party's survival is in doubt? Some of China's leaders are old enough to remember the fateful decisions made in Tiananmen Square in the spring of 1989, a moment when it seemed the fate of their country rested in the balance. If there is another such day, the stakes for the world will be much higher, America's president will again be a bystander, and our biggest foreign policy bet may cost us dearly.

But the biggest problem with the Moneyball approach is that while some governments and peoples might welcome an America that behaves more like an ordinary country and less like an exceptional superpower, there won't be much support for such a cold-blooded foreign policy back home. Americans still prefer Republicans and Democrats to technocrats, particularly when it comes to choosing a president. Most still believe their country is exceptional, even if they don't agree on what makes the country different or how best to protect that difference. We may not want to risk the lives of our sons and daughters and spend our hard-earned dollars to rebuild the lives of others, but the idea of "value over values" runs counter to what Americans want to believe about themselves and their country.

The United States isn't like any other country. It's not simply that the Enlightenment values at the heart of our Constitution demand devotion to a higher calling. We won't play Moneyball, because we aren't the Oakland A's. We're not the underdog who must change the rules to compete with the big boys with fatter wallets. We're the New York Yankees, and we've got the championship banners to prove it. Americans know they can't dominate the world, but they believe their country holds a special place in that world, even if only as an aspiration.*

My Choice

For all these reasons, I choose Independent America. That's the scenario that comes closest to what I believe is best for my country. It will only become more difficult in the years ahead for the United States to play an exceptional role in the world. It's all the more important then that America offer an exceptional example at home. In short, I believe it's time for Americans to redefine our true value for the world.

All choices come with costs. It won't be easy for future presidents to withstand periodic waves of intense pressure from hawks

---

* The author wishes to make clear that he is, and always will be, a die-hard fan of the Boston Red Sox. But he recognizes that, for the moment, the Yankees' storied history makes for the better analogy.

at home and friends abroad to entangle the United States in new foreign conflicts, particularly those that involve allies, traditional rivals, headline-capturing atrocities, or any combination of these. A drive to refocus Washington on domestic priorities will inflict significant damage on relations with allies like Japan, Israel, and Britain. We will forfeit some of the already limited influence we have with China's leaders as they make critical decisions.

But Independent America comes closest to my conception of America's wisest path forward, in part because I believe our leaders will make far fewer costly mistakes if they pay greater heed, not just lip service, to our Constitution. America's founders did not intend to leave questions of war and peace in the hands of the president alone. There are too many lives, too much money, and too many interests at stake. Congress is the guarantor of our security and our liberties. The president, every president, must respect its authority on these questions.

I also believe that our elected leaders must build a foreign policy that can earn strong and lasting public backing. At this moment in our history, the American people will not support costly interference in countries and questions they don't care about, and there is no credible evidence that this trend, reflected in many published polls, will prove short-lived. That's not just because so many Americans no longer believe that their children will live better than they do, an historic shift in U.S. public opinion.[1] It's also because many Americans have come to accept that a stronger will, deeper insight, and deeper pockets will not help us reshape the world as we would like. No nation, not even the sole superpower, can consistently get what it wants in a world where so many other governments have enough power to shrug off U.S. pressure.

In an earlier chapter, I asked what lessons Americans learned in Vietnam. The primary lesson we *should* have learned—and again in Iraq and Afghanistan—is that no matter how powerful you are, it's hard to defeat an enemy that cares much more about the outcome than you do. Why did Washington stumble into an escalating conflict with Russia over Ukraine, a country that will always matter much more to Moscow than to us? The Europeans won't follow our lead indefinitely. We're driving Russia toward China. The Kremlin will find ways to undermine U.S. interests in the Middle East. Russia is too big to isolate. This is not a new Cold War. The American people don't care. So why did we pick this fight? To defend a principle? To "project strength," a fancy way of saying we want to show the world how tough we are? We don't hate or fear Russia. Washington is angry at one particular Russian.

In the Middle East, why do we continue to push Israelis and Palestinians toward a political deal that neither side really wants? Why continue to defend the region's dictators while claiming to defend democracy, freedom, and human rights? Will we continue to confront ISIS, leave it to the local powers directly at risk, or try unsuccessfully to make everyone happy by doing half of what's needed, accomplishing little of lasting value? If we care about the innocents trapped inside those countries, accept them as refugees. "Send these, the homeless, tempest-tossed to me, I lift my lamp beside the golden door!"* That's an American principle, one we can be proud of. Instead, the message too often from Washington is, "Follow our rules or we'll punish you." How did our values become so narrow and stray so far from the America we were taught to love as children?

Over the next ten years, there will be more volatility, more conflict, and more uncertainty, particularly in and around China, and the decisions that that country's leaders make will matter for us all.

---

* From "The New Colossus," the sonnet by Emma Lazarus immortalized on the pedestal of the Statue of Liberty.

But China will build a more open society, or it won't. It will modernize its economy without provoking red-alert levels of social unrest, or it won't. It will partner with the United States on projects of common value, or it won't. China and Japan will avoid conflict, or they won't. Given the uncertainties ahead for this enormous still-developing country, the answers to these questions will play a much larger role in shaping tomorrow's world than any decision made in Washington, and American influence in these decisions won't be nearly as important as our leaders say they believe.

Our country's true promise—for Americans and for the world—depends now on our willingness to lead by example. To champion the Indispensable approach is to ignore the change all around us. To select Moneyball is to cope with that change by sacrificing our values. To embrace Independent America is to find a brave new purpose for those values. Democracy is a process, and the best way to persuade the citizens of other countries to demand democracy from their governments is to make it work much more effectively at home. Don't just tell the world that democracy is best. Show them. Show them that our leaders can move beyond petty partisan fights over legislative leverage to forge the intelligent compromises on which progress always depends.

Instead of throwing money at other people's problems, let's invest more money more wisely in American education, rebuild our infrastructure, care for our veterans and all those who need help here at home, and allow Americans to keep more of what they earn to help build the strong, resilient economy crucial for the country's future. Putting an end to our prohibitively expensive superhero foreign policy can make all that possible. Let our strength, optimism, dynamism, openness, inclusiveness, and innovative spirit serve as our message to the world. This choice represents principles that Republican, Democratic, and independent officials and voters say they care about. Let's build an America that others believe is too important to fail.

These values are not isolationist. We should continue to export things of value, particularly technology, energy, and food. We should welcome citizens of other countries who want to come to America to build a better life for themselves and their families. This is how we will create the world's first truly global workforce— a source of lasting strength. We can continue to offer the world a strong and stable currency. But we must set and maintain an *exceptionally* high bar for political and (especially) military intervention beyond our borders. For the past twenty-five years, we've acted as if we were becoming stronger in the world. We're not, and our foreign policy should reflect that.

We can't renounce important international commitments overnight. Our allies need time to transition to a world in which they must assume greater responsibility for their own security. But only a crystal clear signal from Washington that America will now lead mainly by example will force our traditional partners to stand on their own. Our allies aren't selfish. They're rational. Why should they spend money and accept risks when they believe Washington will do most of it for them? Germany and Japan in particular are wealthy countries that can take responsibility for their own security. Officials in both countries have said publicly that they want to. It will be easier for them to shake their citizens out of their complacency if America makes clear it will do less in years to come. Then our leaders will have to prove that they mean what they say by consistently resisting pressure and temptation to intervene in conflicts that have little bearing on U.S. national security or the strength of our economy. There may one day be greater demand, from the American people and from others, for U.S. international leadership. That day is not on the horizon.

There is one subject on which I strongly disagree with the scenario I described in the Independent America chapter. To capture
the views of many others I've heard championing this vision of the
country's future, I felt a responsibility to give voice to a widely held
trade skepticism that I don't share. I don't believe that a pro-trade
stance is inconsistent with the vision of an America that declares
independence from its superhero foreign policy. In fact, trade is crucial for the continuing strength of alliances that can no longer depend on our military might. Is trade really a job killer? There is
compelling evidence that rising inequality, wage stagnation, and
lost jobs are as much a result of inevitable technological change as
of outsourcing.[2] It's true that the benefits of some recent trade deals
have not been shared as broadly as promised. That's why so many
Americans now oppose new agreements. If ordinary people can see
and feel the benefits of trade, they will support it.

* * * * * * *

But this book is about *your* choice. I hope you now have a clearer
idea of what you believe and why you believe it—and that this book
will help open a much-needed debate on America's future. I also
hope the book has helped persuade you that complex questions
don't yield to simple answers. I know that sounds obvious, but so
much of what Americans see, hear, and read these days is designed
to persuade us that one argument is clearly superior to all others
and that it's a moral outrage that others don't see it that way. Rigid
opinion, self-righteously expressed, whether from liberals or conservatives, has badly damaged our country.

Liberals too often appear to believe that every American problem has a government-driven solution. Conservatives too often advance arguments based mainly on tribal loyalty. We must make

choices. But let's have the courage to accept that there are flaws even in our best arguments and that those who disagree with us have some legitimate points on their side. Our leaders are rarely presented with clear, clean options. Look back at the short quiz you took in the introduction. I bet that you'll find that some of your answers line up with Indispensable arguments, others with Moneyball, and still others with Independent. I hope that a second look makes clear that all three of these arguments have real merits and significant drawbacks. But I also hope you recognize that if you take those questions one at a time, and you try to answer them without a broader strategy in mind, the sum of your answers will create a foreign policy that's impossible to explain—to our allies, our enemies, or the American people. That's what our elected leaders have been doing for years. They've been improvising responses to challenges as they arise without a comprehensive strategy to guide their choices.

If you live long enough, you will face a few difficult personal decisions that set you on a path toward the rest of your life. You've probably already made a few of these big decisions. We guess. We gamble. We close the door on interesting possibilities and hope to discover opportunities we could not have imagined. But if we fail to choose, our choices will be made for us—and we will live with more than our share of regret. America faces a critical choice.

May we choose wisely.

Acknowledgments

I blame you, the reader, for this one. Too many times over the years I've given a talk or an interview on the changing world or a crisis somewhere, and someone wants to know what I think should be done about it. I've always done my best to shrug off these questions. I'm an analyst, not a policymaker. But the questions keep coming, and I've finally decided to have a go.

I don't pretend to have all the answers, and I'm confident that no complex question can ever produce a single comprehensive response. But faced with any important challenge, we each must make decisions. On this most important question—the future of America's role in the world—I've taken my most sincere shot. I hope you will too.

As ever, I've had plenty of help. I'm extremely fortunate to have so many people, friends and colleagues, with whom to share ideas and make them stronger. My respect and gratitude to Vint Cerf, Steve Clemons, Jared Cohen, Ivo Daalder, Ronan Farrow, Catherine Fieschi, Chrystia Freeland, David Fromkin, Ken Griffin, Nikolas Gvosdev, Richard Haass, Guy Hands, Peter Henry, Ken Hersh,

Wolfgang Ischinger, Bob Kagan, Zachary Karabell, Tom Keene, Parag Khanna, Sallie Krawcheck, Martina Larkin, Mark Leonard, David Lipton, Maziar Minovi, Niko Pfund, Doug and Heidi Rediker, Joel Rosenthal, Alec Ross, Nouriel Roubini, Josette Sheeran, Marci Shore, Doug Shuman, Martin Sorrell, Nick Thompson, Enzo Viscusi, Fareed Zakaria, and Bob Zoellick.

Policy leaders, both inside and outside the U.S. government, current and recent, have fueled this work with their ideas and concerns. Heartfelt thanks to Madeleine Albright, John Baird, Carl Bildt, Mark Carney, Martin Dempsey, Ho Ching, Jon Huntsman, Yoriko Kawaguchi, Christine Lagarde, David Miliband, George Osborne, Corrado Passera, Vladimir Putin, Javier Solana, Jim Stavridis, and Larry Summers. Just kidding about Putin.

There are so many interesting and insightful books about American foreign policy, but I'd like to single out two that were especially useful for me in trying to capture the voices of Independent, Moneyball, and Indispensable America. They are *Special Providence: American Foreign Policy and How It Changed the World* by Walter Russell Mead and *Ethical Realism: A Vision for America's Role in the World* by Anatol Lieven and John Hulsman.

My career as a writer and thinker has been thoroughly intertwined with Eurasia Group and its brilliant team of analysts. I hope our modest efforts at a behavioral revolution in political science are making a difference in the field; they've added immeasurably to my understanding of the world. The whole research team deserves my appreciation for their contributions to *Superpower*. In particular, Corey Boles, Nick Consonery, Chris Garman, David Gordon, Robert Johnston, Alex Kazan, Dan Kerner, Cliff Kupchan, Philippe de Pontet, Greg Priddy, Mij Rahman, Divya Reddy, Mark Rosenberg, Kevin Rudd, Hani Sabra, Scott Seaman, and Sean West have provided crucial support.

ACKNOWLEDGMENTS

You don't mess with Willis Sparks. We've worked together for ten years and five books. It feels like we've built our careers together; my work has benefited immensely from Willis's being part of it, and our collaboration is only getting deeper. Mike Sard keeps both of us honest and on point, and he's thoroughly impossible not to like. Not sure about his new beard, though. Sincere thanks to Sarah Lorch and Jake Miner for consistently smart research support.

Alex Sanford, my indispensable marketing and media maven, always looks at the big picture, and it's fun and gratifying to work with her. The fearsome Jenna Rosebery, the small (but dangerous) Kim Tran, and the wonkily incisive Matt Peterson keep me moving, well informed, on time, and sane.

To my publishing team: Adrian Zackheim embraces his inner curmudgeon in a way that I find aspirational; I think he has come to like me in spite of himself. We're both fortunate to be working with Will Weisser, Emily Angell, Tara Gilbride, and Brittany Wienke at Portfolio. So too our strategically brilliant publicists, Allison McLean and Liz Hazelton of Amplify Partners. Finally, the super-solid Rafe Sagelyn, my agent, to whom I've now (successfully!) introduced a small handful of talented authors. Many thanks, Rafe.

And to my chickie, Ann, my brother, Rob, and my dog, Moose. You deserve better. But only a little.

New York
February 2015

NOTES

Preface

xvi Mike Allen and Daniel Lippman, "Trump's 'America First' Positions Him to Left of Hillary—*Politico Magazine* Media Issue: Ben 'This Guy' Schreckinger on What It's like to Cover Trump—Andrew Ross Sorkin: Why Obama Is Frustrated," Politico.com, April 28, 2016, http://www.politico.com/playbook/2016/04/trumps-america-first-positions-him-to-left-of-hillary-politico-magazine-media-issue-ben-this-guy-schreckinger-on-what-its-like-to-cover-trump-andrew-ross-sorkin-why-obama-is-frustrated-214003.

Chapter 1: Today's World and Tomorrow's

1 United States Census Bureau, "Exhibit 6. Exports, Imports, and Trade Balance by Country and Area, Not Seasonally Adjusted: 2014," census.gov, http://www.census.gov/foreign-trade/Press-Release/2014pr/12/exh6s.pdf.

2 European Commission, "Trade > Policy > Countries and Regions > Russia," ec.europa.eu, April 26, 2016, http://ec.europa.eu/trade/policy/countries-and-regions/countries/russia/.

3 "Data Protection: Angela Merkel Proposes Europe Network," BBC

News, February 15, 2014, http://www.bbc.com/news/world-europe
-26210053.

4 Jim Yardley and Gardiner Harris, "2nd Day of Power Failures Cripples Wide Swath of India," *New York Times,* July 31, 2012, http://www
.nytimes.com/2012/08/01/world/asia/power-outages-hit-600-million
-in-india.html?pagewanted=all&_r=0.

5 Jonathan Watts, "Brazil Protests Erupt over Public Services and
World Cup Costs," *Guardian,* June 18, 2013, http://www.theguardian
.com/world/2013/jun/18/brazil-protests-erupt-huge-scale; Simon
Romero, "Thousands Gather for Protests in Brazil's Largest Cities,"
New York Times, June 17, 2013, http://www.nytimes.com/2013/06/18/
world/americas/thousands-gather-for-protests-in-brazils-largest-cities
.html?_r=0.

6 Anushay Hossain, "Beyond the Sycamore Trees: What the Turkey
Protests Really Represent," *Forbes,* June 9, 2013, http://www.forbes
.com/sites/worldviews/2013/06/09/beyond-the-sycamore-trees-what
-the-turkey-protests-really-represent/.

7 See Daniel W. Drezner's book *The System Worked: How the World
Stopped Another Great Depression* (New York: Oxford University Press,
2014).

8 Peter Apps, "East-West Military Gap Rapidly Shrinking: Report,"
Reuters, March 8, 2011, http://www.reuters.com/article/2011/03/08/us
-world-military-idUSTRE7273UB20110308.

9 Thomas E. Donilon, the Landon Lecture, Council on Foreign Relations, April 14, 2014, http://www.cfr.org/united-states/landon-lecture/
p32846.

10 Robert Farley, "Does the U.S. Navy Have 10 or 19 Aircraft Carriers?"
The Diplomat, April 17, 2014, http://thediplomat.com/2014/04/does
-the-us-navy-have-10-or-19-aircraft-carriers/.

11 The best example was French president Charles de Gaulle's decision in
1966 to withdraw France from NATO's military structures and expel
NATO troops from French territory.

12 "An Acronym with Capital," *Economist,* July 19, 2014, http://www
.economist.com/news/finance-and-economics/21607851-setting-up
-rivals-imf-and-world-bank-easier-running-them-acronym; Chris
Hogg, "China Banks Lend More Than World Bank—Report," BBC
News, January 18, 2011, http://www.bbc.com/news/world-asia-pacific
-12212936.

13 Peter Wong, "Renminbi Challenging US Dollar Hegemony as Global
Economic Gravity Moves East," *The Nation* (Thailand), September 2,
2014, http://www.nationmultimedia.com/business/Renminbi
-challenging-US-dollar-hegemony-as-global--30242259.html.

14 Pew Research Center for the People and the Press, "Public See U.S. Power Declining as Support for Global Engagement Slips," December 3, 2013, http://www.people-press.org/2013/12/03/public-sees-u-s -power-declining-as-support-for-global-engagement-slips/.

15 Charlie Campbell, "Germany, Brazil Take NSA Spying Gripes to U.S.," *Time,* October 25, 2013, http://world.time.com/2013/10/25/ germany-brazil-take-nsa-spying-gripes-to-u-n/.

16 International Monetary Fund, "World Economic Outlook Database, April 2015," IMF.org, April 2015, http://www.imf.org/external/pubs/ft/ weo/2015/01/weodata/weorept.aspx?pr.x=69.

17 U.S. Chamber of Commerce, "The Benefits of International Trade," https://www.uschamber.com/international/international-policy/ benefits-international-trade-0.

18 "Trading Up" (editorial), *National Review,* July 9, 2010, http://www .nationalreview.com/articles/243435/trading-editors.

19 Donilon, Landon Lecture.

20 See the following examples: Barack Obama, "Remarks by the President on America's Energy Security" (March 30, 2011), White House, Office of the Press Secretary, http://www.whitehouse.gov/the-press -office/2011/03/30/remarks-president-americas-energy-security; George W. Bush, "State of the Union Address" (January 23, 2007), White House, http://georgewbush-whitehouse.archives.gov/news/releases/ 2007/01/20070123-2.html; Bill Clinton, "The President's Radio Address" (March 18, 2000), American Presidency Project, http://www .presidency.ucsb.edu/ws/index.php?pid=58262; George H. W. Bush, "Remarks at a Briefing on Energy Policy" (February 20, 1991), American Presidency Project, http://www.presidency.ucsb.edu/ws/index .php?pid=19318&st=energy+policy&st1=; Ronald Reagan, "Statement on Signing the Energy Emergency Preparedness Act of 1982" (August 3, 1982), American Presidency Project, http://www.presidency.ucsb .edu/ws/index.php?pid=42816&st=foreign+oil&st1=; Jimmy Carter, "Energy Address to the Nation" (April 5, 1979), American Presidency Project, http://www.presidency.ucsb.edu/ws/index.php?pid=32159&st= Iran&st1=; Gerald Ford, "Address to the Nation on Energy Programs" (May 27, 1975), American Presidency Project, http://www.presidency. ucsb.edu/ws/index.php?pid=4942&st=foreign+oil&st1=; Richard Nixon, "The President's News Conference" (February 25, 1974), Miller Center, http://millercenter.org/president/nixon/speeches/speech-3888.

21 Grant Smith, "U.S. Seen as Biggest Oil Producer After Overtaking Saudi," Bloomberg.com, July 4, 2014, http://www.bloomberg.com/ news/articles/2014-07-04/u-s-seen-as-biggest-oil-producer-after -overtaking-saudi; Chris Isidore, "U.S. Could Be Energy Independent

Within Four Years," Money.CNN.com, April 15, 2015, http://money
.cnn.com/2015/04/15/investing/us-energy-independence.

22   Central Intelligence Agency, "The World Factbook," CIA.gov, 2016–
2017, https://www.cia.gov/library/publications/the-world-factbook/
fields/2177.html.

23   UN Department of Economic and Social Affairs, *World Population
Prospects: The 2012 Revision,* http://esa.un.org/wpp/Documentation/
pdf/WPP2012_HIGHLIGHTS.pdf.

24   Gayle Smith, "U.S. Global Development Lab Launches to Develop
and Scale Solutions to Global Challenges," USAID, April 4, 2014,
http://blog.usaid.gov/2014/04/u-s-global-development-lab-launches-to
-develop-and-scale-solutions-to-global-challenges/.

Chapter 2: Incoherent America

1   Gorbachev's December 7, 1988, speech at the United Nations is widely
available online; for a written transcript of excerpts of the speech, see
http://astro.temple.edu/~rimmerma/gorbachev_speech_to_UN.htm.

2   George H. W. Bush, "Address Before a Joint Session of Congress"
(September 11, 1990), Miller Center, http://millercenter.org/president/
bush/speeches/speech-3425.

3   George H. W. Bush quoted in Kate Aurthur, " 'In a Few Days, the
Mood Shifted: Why Hadn't We Won Yet?' " *New York Times,* March
23, 2003, http://www.nytimes.com/2003/03/23/weekinreview/
23WORD.html.

4   William J. Clinton, "Address Before a Joint Session of Congress on
Administration Goals" (February 17, 1993), American Presidency
Project, http://www.presidency.ucsb.edu/ws/index.php?pid=
47232&st=Peace+Dividend&st1=.

5   Mary Elise Sarotte, "Enlarging NATO, Expanding Confusion," *New
York Times,* November 29, 2009, http://www.nytimes.com/2009/11/30/
opinion/30sarotte.html?pagewanted=all&_r=0.

6   World Bank, "GDP Per Capita (Current US$)," http://data.worldbank
.org/indicator/NY.GDP.PCAP.CD?page=2.

7   By the end of the Clinton administration, "Who lost Russia?" was a
widely debated question in the United States. Robert D. Kaplan, "Who
Lost Russia?" (review of Stephen F. Cohen, *Failed Crusade: America and
the Tragedy of Post-Communist Russia*), *New York Times,* October 8, 2000,
http://www.nytimes.com/2000/10/08/books/who-lost-russia.html.

8   U.S. Department of State, "China: WTP Accession and Permanent
Normal Trade Relations (PNTR)," May 24, 2000, http://www.state
.gov/1997-2001-NOPDFS/regions/eap/fs-china_pntr-wto_000524.html.

9   "Between Hope and History: On Free Trade," http://www.ontheissues .org/Archive/Hope_+_History_Free_Trade.htm.

10   Martin Kelly, "Top 15 Presidential Campain Slogans," *About Education,* http://americanhistory.about.com/od/elections/tp/Top-15 -Presidential-Campaign-Slogans.htm.

11   Louis Jacobson, "Hillary Clinton Says Economic Stats Were 100 Times Better Under Clinton Than Ronald Reagan," *PolitiFact,* July 21, 2014, http://www.politifact.com/truth-o-meter/statements/2014/ jul/21/hillary-clinton/hillary-clinton-says-economic-stats-were-100 -times/.

12   "Presidential Debate Excerpts: Gov. George W. Bush vs. Vice President Al Gore" (October 12, 2000), *PBS NewsHour,* http://www.pbs .org/newshour/bb/politics-july-dec00-for-policy_10-12/.

13   "Presidential Debate in Winston-Salem, North Carolina" (October 11, 2000), American Presidency Project, http://www.presidency.ucsb.edu/ ws/?pid=29419.

14   Joe Klein, "It's Time for Extreme Peacekeeping," *Time,* November 16, 2003, http://content.time.com/time/nation/article/0,8599,543748,00.html.

15   The figure quoted here is in 2013 dollars. Sue Owen, "Obamacare Law Was 'Funded' and Expected to Save Billions; Not So for Medicare Part D," *PolitiFact,* November 18, 2013, http://www.politifact .com/texas/statements/2013/nov/18/facebook-posts/obamacare-law -was-funded-and-expected-save-billion/.

16   Pew Research Global Attitudes Project, "Global Public Opinion in the Bush Years (2001–2008)," December 18, 2008, http://www.pewglobal .org/2008/12/18/global-public-opinion-in-the-bush-years-2001-2008/.

17   Special Inspector General for Afghan Reconstruction, *Quarterly Report to the United States Congress,* July 30, 2014, http://www.sigar.mil/ pdf/quarterlyreports/2014-07-30qr.pdf.

18   Embassy of the United States, London, "Delivering on the Promise of Economic Statecraft," November 17, 2012, http://london.usembassy .gov/forpol348.html.

19   "Obama's Blurry Red Line," FactCheck.org, September 6, 2013, http:// www.factcheck.org/2013/09/obamas-blurry-red-line/.

20   "Gaza-Israel Conflict: Is the Fighting Over?" BBC News, August 26, 2014, http://www.bbc.com/news/world-middle-east-28252155; "Gaza Crisis: Toll of Operations in Gaza," BBC News, September 1, 2014, http://www.bbc.com/news/world-middle-east-28439404.

21   See Princeton University Press's page for their edition of his writings, *Carl von Clausewitz: Historical and Political Writings,* http://press .princeton.edu/titles/4876.html.

Chapter 3: Independent America

1　Angela Young, "Global Defense Budget Seen Climbing in 2014; First Total Increase Since 2009 as Russia Surpasses Britain and Saudi Arabia Continues Its Security Spending Spree," *International Business Times,* February 6, 2014, http://www.ibtimes.com/global-defense-budget-seen -climbing-2014-first-total-increase-2009-russia-surpasses-britain-saudi.

2　The Eisenhower Project, http://www.eisenhowerproject.org/.

3　The Concord Coalition, "What Is the Total U.S. National Debt?," concordcoalition.org, June 9, 2016, http://www.concordcoalition.org/ issues/indicators/what-total-us-national-debt.

4　Scott McConnell, "Bob Gates's Farewell Warning," *American Conservative,* January 21, 2014, http://www.theamericanconservative.com/ bob-gatess-farewell-warning/.

5　Kiran Dhillon, "Afghanistan Is the Big Winner in U.S. Foreign Aid," *Time,* March 31, 2014, http://time.com/43836/afghanistan-is-the-big -winner-in-u-s-foreign-aid/.

6　"Obama Proposes 18 Percent Drop in Aid to Pakistan for Fiscal 2015," *The Nation,* March 7, 2014, http://www.nation.com.pk/national/07 -Mar-2014/obama-proposes-18-drop-in-aid-to-pakistan-for-fiscal-2015.

7　"1914–1918—Casualty Figures," http://www.worldwar1.com/tlcrates .htm.

8　Derek W. Urwin, *A Political History of Western Europe Since 1945,* 5th ed. (New York: Routledge, 1997).

9　William Manchester, *American Caesar: Douglas MacArthur, 1880–1964* (New York: Little, Brown, 1978).

10　Urwin, *A Political History.*

11　William H. Chafe, *The Unfinished Journey: America Since World War II,* 4th ed. (New York: Oxford University Press, 1991).

12　Robert Skidelsky, *John Maynard Keynes: Fighting for Britain, 1937–1946* (London: Macmillan, 2000).

13　Chafe, *The Unfinished Journey.*

14　Center on Budget and Policy Priorities, "Policy Basics: Where Do Our Federal Tax Dollars Go?" http://www.cbpp.org/cms/?fa=view&id=1258.

15　Pew Research Global Attitudes Project, "Global Opinion of Obama Slips, International Policies Faulted," June 13, 2012, http://www.pew global.org/2012/06/13/global-opinion-of-obama-slips-international -policies-faulted/.

16　Stephen Calabria, "Americans Conflicted About Which NATO Countries They'd Defend from Russia: Poll," *Huffington Post,* April 1, 2014, http://www.huffingtonpost.com/2014/04/01/americans-nato -poll_n_5069838.html.

17   Helene Cooper and Steven Erlanger, "Military Cuts Render NATO Less Formidable as Deterrent to Russia," *New York Times,* March 26, 2014, http://www.nytimes.com/2014/03/27/world/europe/military-cuts -render-nato-less-formidable-as-deterrent-to-russia.html?_r=0; Donald Kirk, "Okinawa Vote Rebuffs Japan, U.S. Plans for Marine Base," *Forbes,* January 19, 2014, http://www.forbes.com/sites/donaldkirk/ 2014/01/19/okinawa-vote-rebuffs-japan-u-s-plans-for-marine-base/.

18   For fuller treatment of these ideas, see Anatol Lieven and John Hulsman, *Ethical Realism: A Vision for America's Role in the World* (New York: Pantheon, 2006).

19   "Q&A: International Criminal Court," BBC News, March 11, 2013, http://www.bbc.com/news/world-11809908.

20   "Hugo Chávez: The Chávez Presidency," *Encyclopaedia Britannica,* http://www.britannica.com/EBchecked/topic/108140/Hugo-Chavez/ 285482/The-Chavez-presidency.

21   Pew Research Center for the People and the Press, "Public See U.S. Power Declining as Support for Global Engagement Slips," December 3, 2013, http://www.people-press.org/2013/12/03/public-sees-u-s-power -declining-as-support-for-global-engagement-slips/.

22   "Madison Argued That War Is the Major Way by Which the Executive Office Increases Its Power, Patronage, and Taxing Power (1793)," Portable Library of Liberty, November 30, 2009, http://files.libertyfund .org/pll/quotes/236.html.

23   Quoted in "The Founding Fathers on the Constitution's War Power," War and Law League, http://warandlaw.homestead.com/files/ foundin2.html.

24   Ibid.

25   Linda J. Blimes, Abstract, "The Financial Legacy of Iraq and Afghanistan: How Wartime Spending Decisions Will Constrain Future National Security Budgets," HKS Faculty Research Working Paper Series RWP13-006, March 2013, https://research.hks.harvard.edu/ publications/workingpapers/citation.aspx?PubId=8956&type=WPN.

26   Public Citizen, *NAFTA's 2-Year Legacy and the Fate of the Trans-Pacific Partnership,* February 2014, http://www.citizen.org/documents/ NAFTA-at-20.pdf.

27   http://www.citizen.org/pressroom/pressroomredirect.cfm?ID=4050.

28   http://angusreid.org/americans-and-canadians-feel-they-have-lost-out -with-nafta/.

29   The evidence points overwhelmingly to the conclusion that Mexico's reforms, backed by NAFTA, have largely been a disappointment for the country. Despite dramatic increases in trade and foreign investment, economic growth has been slow and job creation has been weak.

30   Thomas L. Friedman and Michael Mandelbaum, *That Used to Be Us: How America Fell Behind in the World It Invented and How We Can Come Back* (New York: Farrar, Straus & Giroux, 2011).

31   American Society of Civil Engineers (ASCE), "2013 Report Card for America's Infrastructure," http://www.infrastructurereportcard.org/a/#p/home. Subcategories: "Aviation," http://www.infrastructurereport card.org/a/#p/aviation/overview; "Transit," http://www.infrastructure reportcard.org/a/#p/transit/overview; "Roads," http://www.infrastructure reportcard.org/a/#p/roads/overview.

32   Ibid., "Schools," http://www.infrastructurereportcard.org/a/#p/schools/overview.

33   Allie Bidwell, "American Students Fall in International Academic Tests, Chinese Lead the Pack," *USA Today,* December 3, 2013, http://www.usnews.com/news/articles/2013/12/03/american-students-fall-in-international-academic-tests-chinese-lead-the-pack.

34   Tim Walker, "International Study Links Higher Teacher Pay and Teacher Quality," *neaToday,* January 4, 2012, http://neatoday.org/2012/01/04/international-study-links-higher-teacher-pay-and-student-performance/.

35   Agence France-Presse, "Study: Iraq, Afghan Wars to Cost U.S. Up to $6 Trillion," *Defense News,* March 29, 2013, http://www.defensenews.com/article/20130329/DEFREG02/303290018/Study-Iraq-Afghan-Wars-Cost-U-S-Up-6-Trillion.

36   Colonel Jack Jacobs, U.S. Army (Ret.), "Want to Fix VA Health Care? Get Rid of It," ABC News, May 14, 2014, http://www.nbcnews.com/storyline/va-hospital-scandal/want-fix-va-health-care-get-rid-it-n106601.

Chapter 4: Moneyball America

1   U.S. Energy Information Administration, "World Oil Transit Choke-points," http://www.eia.gov/countries/regions-topics.cfm?fips=wotc&trk=p3.

2   "Strait of Hormuz: The World's Key Oil Choke Point," *National Geographic,* http://environment.nationalgeographic.com/environment/energy/great-energy-challenge/strait-of-hormuz/.

3   U.S. Energy Information Administration, "Five States and the Gulf of Mexico Produce More Than 80% of U.S. Crude Oil," March 31, 2014, http://www.eia.gov/todayinenergy/detail.cfm?id=15631.

4   Grant Smith, "U.S. Seen as Biggest Oil Producer After Overtaking Saudi," Bloomberg.com, July 4, 2014, http://www.bloomberg.com/news/articles/2014-07-04/u-s-seen-as-biggest-oil-producer-after

-overtaking-saudi; Chris Isidore, "U.S. Could Be Energy Independent Within Four Years," Money.CNN.com, April 15, 2015, http://money .cnn.com/2015/04/15/investing/us-energy-independence.

5   Michael Lewis, *Moneyball: The Art of Winning an Unfair Game* (New York: Norton, 2003).

6   Jeffrey Goldberg, "Breaking Ranks," *New Yorker*, October 31, 2005, http://www.newyorker.com/magazine/2005/10/31/breaking-ranks.

7   Council on Foreign Relations, "Profile: Osama bin Laden," http:// www.cfr.org/terrorist-leaders/profile-osama-bin-laden/p9951#p6.

8   Anna Fifield, "Contractors Reap $138bn from Iraq War," *Financial Times*, March 18, 2013, http://www.ft.com/cms/s/0/7f435f04-8c05-11e2 -b001-00144feabdc0.html#axzz3HN0d1Has.

9   Costs of War, http://costsofwar.org/.

10 David W. Moore, "Americans Believe U.S. Participation in Gulf War a Decade Ago Worthwhile," Gallup, February 26, 2001, http://www .gallup.com/poll/1963/amer . . . orthwhile.aspx.

11 "Iraq . . . and ISIS," PollingReport.com, November 21–23, 2014, http:// www.pollingreport.com/iraq.htm.

12 "Iraq War Illegal, Says Annan," BBC News, September 16, 2004, http://news.bbc.co.uk/2/hi/world/middle_east/3661134.stm.

13 "Beirut Marine Barracks Bombing Fast Facts," CNN, http://www .cnn.com/2013/06/13/world/meast/beirut-marine-barracks-bombing -fast-facts/.

14 "Interview: Caspar Weinberger," *Frontline*, September 2001, http:// www.pbs.org/wgbh/pages/frontline/shows/target/interviews/weinberger .html.

15 See Anatol Lieven and John Hulsman, *Ethical Realism: A Vision for America's Role in the World* (New York: Pantheon, 2006), 122–23, though the idea of sustaining regional balances of power to keep the peace is an idea much older than the United States of America.

16 Ibid., 3.

17 Craig Whitlock, "U.S. Expands Secret Intelligence Operations in Africa," *Washington Post*, June 13, 2012, http://www.washingtonpost.com/ world/national-security/us-expands-secret-intelligence-operations-in -africa/2012/06/13/gJQAHyvAbV_story.html.

18 Ryan Lizza, "The Consequentialist: How the Arab Spring Remade Obama's Foreign Policy," *New Yorker*, May 2, 2011, http://www.new yorker.com/magazine/2011/05/02/the-consequentialist.

19 Ivo H. Daalder and James G. Stavridis, "NATO's Success in Libya," *New York Times*, October 30, 2011, http://www.nytimes.com/ 2011/10/31/opinion/31iht-eddaalder31.html?_r=1&.

20 "Press Briefing by Press Secretary Jay Carney" (October 20, 2011),

White House, http://www.whitehouse.gov/the-press-office/2011/10/20/
press-briefing-press-secretary-jay-carney.

21 Raphael Cohen and Gabriel Scheinmann, "Lessons from Libya:
America Can't Lead from Behind," *Time*, February 15, 2014, http://
ideas.time.com/2014/02/15/lessons-from-libya-america-cant-lead-from
-behind/.

22 For a fuller explanation of this idea, see my book *The J Curve: A New
Way to Understand Why Nations Rise and Fall* (New York: Simon &
Schuster, 2007).

23 U.S. Energy Information Administration, "Japan," http://www.eia
.gov/countries/cab.cfm?fips=JA.

24 Christina Larson, "Water Shortages Will Limit Global Shale Gas Development, Especially in China," *Bloomberg Businessweek,* September
2, 2014, http://www.businessweek.com/articles/2014-09-02/water
-shortages-will-limit-global-shale-gas-development-especially-in-china.

25 Kevin Granville, "The Trans-Pacific Partnership Trade Accord Ex-
plained," *New York Times*, October 5, 2015, http://www.nytimes.com
/2015/10/06/business/international/the-trans-pacific-partnership-trade
-deal-explained.html.

26 Richard Rosecrance, *The Rise of the Trading State: Commerce and Conquest in the Modern World* (New York: Basic Books, 1986).

27 See Lieven and Hulsman, *Ethical Realism.*

28 Rosecrance, *The Rise of the Trading State.*

29 UN Conference on Trade and Development (UNCTAD), "World
Investment Report 2015: Reforming International Investment Governance," June 24, 2015, http://unctad.org/en/PublicationsLibrary/
wir2015_en.pdf.

30 William H. Chafe, *The Unfinished Journey: America Since World War
II*, 4th ed. (New York: Oxford University Press, 1991).

31 "Marshall Plan," Digital History, http://www.digitalhistory.uh.edu/
disp_textbook.cfm?smtID=3&psid=4077.

32 Urwin, *A Political History.*

33 Lieven and Hulsman, *Ethical Realism,* 80–83.

Chapter 5: Indispensable America

1 China passed the United States as the world's biggest trading nation,
as measured by the sum of exports and imports, in 2012 after six decades of U.S. dominance. "China Overtakes US as World's Largest
Trading Country," RT.com, February 11, 2013, http://rt.com/business/
china-us-largest-trading-country-908/.

2 Ted Plafker, "A Year Later, China's Stimulus Package Bears Fruit,"

New York Times, October 22, 2009, http://www.nytimes.com/2009/ 10/23/business/global/23iht-rglobalchin.html?pagewanted=all&_r=0.

3   Centers for Disease Control and Prevention, "Severe Acute Respiratory Syndrome (SARS)," http://www.cdc.gov/sars/; ibid., "Fact Sheet: Basic Information About SARS," http://www.cdc.gov/sars/about/fs -SARS.pdf.

4   World Health Organization, "Cumulative Number of Confirmed Cases of Avian Influenza A (H5N1) Reported to WHO," http://www .who.int/influenza/human_animal_interface/H5N1_cumulative_ table_archives/en/; "H5N1 Avian Flu (H5N1 Bird Flu)," Flu.gov, http://www.flu.gov/about_the_flu/h5n1/.

5   "Ebola in Africa: The End of a Tragedy?" *Economist,* January 14, 2016, http://www.economist.com/blogs/graphicdetail/2015/08/ebola -graphics.

6   For a fuller treatment of this idea, see my book *The J Curve: A New Way to Understand Why Nations Rise and Fall* (New York: Simon & Schuster, 2007).

7   For a more detailed discussion of both the North Korea and climate opportunities in U.S.-Chinese relations, see Bruce Jentleson, "Strategic Recalibration: Framework for a 21st-Century National Security Strategy," *Washington Quarterly,* March 1, 2014, http://twq.elliott.gwu.edu/ strategic-recalibration-framework-21st-century-national-security -strategy.

8   International Monetary Fund, "World Economic Outlook Database, April 2015," IMF.org, April 2015, http://www.imf.org/external/pubs/ft/ weo/2016/01/weodata/weorept.aspx?pr.x=55&pr.y=11&sy=1989&ey= 2015&scsm=1&ssd=1&sort=country&ds=.&br=1&c=964%2C926&s=PPP PC&grp=0&a.

9   Oxfam, "Foreign Aid 101: A Quick and Easy Guide to Understanding US Foreign Aid," http://www.oxfamamerica.org/explore/research -publications/forcign-aid-101/.

10 International Monetary Fund, "About the IMF," https://www.imf.org/ external/about.htm.

11 Ibid., "History," http://www.imf.org/external/about/history.htm; ibid., "Our Work," http://www.imf.org/external/about/ourwork.htm.

12 For an excellent elaboration of the history of democracy promotion in U.S. foreign policy, see Walter Russell Mead, *Special Providence: American Foreign Policy and How It Changed the World* (New York: Knopf, 2001), chapter 5: "The Connecticut Yankee in the Court of King Arthur: Wilsonianism and Its Mission."

13 Ivan Perkins, "Why Don't Democracies Fight Each Other?" *Washington Post,* June 20, 2014, http://www.washingtonpost.com/news/volokh

-conspiracy/wp/2014/06/20/by-ivan-perkins-why-dont-democracies
-fight-each-other/.

14 "List of Countries by GDP (PPP) Per Capita," Wikipedia, http://
en.wikipedia.org/wiki/List_of_countries_by_GDP_(PPP)_per_capita.

15 International Monetary Fund, "World Economic Outlook Database,
April 2015," IMF.org, April 2015, http://www.imf.org/external/pubs/ft/
weo/2016/01/weodata/weorept.aspx?sy=2012&ey=2017&scsm=1&ssd
=1&sort=country&ds=.&br=1&prl.x=38&prl.y=13&c=512,672,914,946,
612,137,614,546,311,962,213,674,911,676,193,548,122,556,912,678,313,
181,419,867,513,682,316,684,913,273,124,868,339,921,638,948,514,943,
218,686,963,688,616,518,223,728,516,558,918,138,748,196,618,278,624,
692,522,694,622,142,156,449,626,564,628,565,228,283,924,853,233,288,
632,293,636,566,634,964,238,182,662,359,960,453,423,968,935,922,128,
714,611,862,321,135,243,716,248,456,469,722,253,942,642,718,643,724,
939,576,644,936,819,961,172,813,132,199,646,733,648,184,915,524,134,
361,652,362,174,364,328,732,258,366,656,734,654,144,336,146,263,463,
268,528,532,923,944,738,176,578,534,537,536,742,429,866,433,369,178,
744,436,186,136,925,343,869,158,746,439,926,916,466,664,112,826,111,
542,298,967,927,443,846,917,299,544,582,941,474,446,754,666,698,668&s
=NGDPDPC&grp=0&a=.

16 For a broader discussion of democracy promotion, see Sean M. Jones,
"Why the United States Should Spread Democracy," Discussion Paper
98-07, Center for Science and International Affairs, Harvard University, March 1998, http://belfercenter.ksg.harvard.edu/publication/2830/
why_the_united_states_should_spread_democracy.html.

Chapter 6: Question Mark America

1 "Remarks by the President at the Air Force Academy Commence-
ment" (May 23, 2012), White House, http://www.whitehouse.gov/the
-press-office/2012/05/23/remarks-president-air-force-academy
-commencement.

2 "Weekly Address: A Better Bargain for the Middle Class" (July 27,
2013), White House, http://www.whitehouse.gov/the-press-office/
2013/07/27/weekly-address-better-bargain-middle-class.

3 Mike Allen, "'Don't Do Stupid Sh—' (Stuff)," *Politico,* June 1, 2014,
http://www.politico.com/story/2014/06/dont-do-stupid-shit-president
-obama-white-house-107293.html.

4 Jeffrey Goldberg, "Hillary Clinton: 'Failure' to Help Syrian Rebels Led
to the Rise of ISIS," *Atlantic,* August 10, 2014, http://www.theatlantic
.com/international/archive/2014/08/hillary-clinton-failure-to-help
-syrian-rebels-led-to-the-rise-of-isis/375832/.

5   Mark Landler, "Obama Could Replace Aides Bruised by a Cascade of
     Crises," *New York Times,* October 29, 2014, http://www.nytimes
     .com/2014/10/30/world/middleeast/mounting-crises-raise-questions-on
     -capacity-of-obamas-team.html?hp&action=click&pgtype=Homepage
     &module=first-column-region&region=top-news&WT.nav=top
     -news&_r=1.

6   Jane Perlez, "China and Russia Reach 30-Year Gas Deal," *New York
     Times,* May 21, 2014, http://www.nytimes.com/2014/05/22/world/asia/
     china-russia-gas-deal.html?_r=0.

7   Tim Hanrahan, "Obama Transcript: NATO Will Defend Estonia,
     Latvia, Lithuania," *Wall Street Journal,* September 3, 2014, http://blogs
     .wsj.com/washwire/2014/09/03/obama-transcript-nato-will-defend
     -estonia-latvia-lithuania/.

8   Reynolds Holding, "U.S. Justice Seems to Fall Harder on Foreign
     Companies," *New York Times,* July 1, 2014, http://dealbook.nytimes
     .com/2014/07/01/u-s-justice-seems-to-fall-harder-on-foreign
     -companies/?_php=true&_type=blogs&_r=0; "Capital Punishment:
     France's Largest Bank Gets Fined for Evading American Sanctions,"
     Economist, July 5, 2014, http://www.economist.com/news/finance-and
     -economics/21606321-frances-largest-bank-gets-fined-evading
     -american-sanctions-capital-punishment; Kara Scannell, "BNP Pleads
     Guilty to Sanctions Violations and Faces $8.9bn Fine," *Financial
     Times,* June 30, 2014, http://www.ft.com/intl/cms/s/0/db2daede-009c
     -11e4-9a62-00144feab7de.html#axzz3I2ILAhW1; "US Mortgage Giant
     Attacks UBS and Credit Suisse," SWI, November 1, 2013, http://www
     .swissinfo.ch/eng/us-mortgage-giant-attacks-ubs-and-credit
     -suisse/37241690; Halah Touryalai, "Tale of Two Swiss Banks: Why
     Wegelin Failed and UBS Survived Tax Evasion Charges," *Forbes,* Jan-
     uary 4, 2013, http://www.forbes.com/sites/halahtouryalai/2013/01/04/
     tale-of-two-swiss-banks-why-wegelin-failed-and-ubs-survived-tax
     -evasion-charges/.

9   Michael R. Gordon and Kareem Fahim, "Kerry Says Egypt's Military
     Was 'Restoring Democracy' in Ousting Morsi," *New York Times,* Au-
     gust 1, 2013, http://www.nytimes.com/2013/08/02/world/middleeast/
     egypt-warns-morsi-supporters-to-end-protests.html?_r=1&.

10   "Obama's Blurry Red Line," FactCheck.org., September 6, 2013, http://
     www.factcheck.org/2013/09/obamas-blurry-red-line/.

11   According to the Theodore Roosevelt Center at Dickinson State Uni-
     versity, "this statement is often attributed to Theodore Roosevelt, but
     no known source can be found to verify the attribution."

Conclusion

1 Chris Cillizza, "The Single Most Depressing Number in the New NBC–Wall Street Journal Poll," *Washington Post,* August 6, 2014, http://www.washingtonpost.com/blogs/the-fix/wp/2014/08/06/the -single-most-depressing-number-in-the-new-nbc-wall-street-journal -poll/.
2 David Rolman, "How Technology Is Destroying Jobs," *MIT Technology Review,* June 12, 2013, http://www.technologyreview.com/featured story/515926/how-technology-is-destroying-jobs/.

INDEX